CW00518793

THE COMPLETE ELECTRIC BASS PLAYER

BY CHUCK RAINEY

BOOK 1: THE METHOD

Amsco Publications
New York/London/Sydney/Cologne

Edited by Ronnie Ball and Antonio Fernandez
Interior design by The Bookmakers, Incorporated
Interior photography by Leonard Vogler
Music engraving by WR Music Service
Cover design by Pearce Marchbank
Cover photography by Rod Shone

Copyright © 1985 by Amsco Publications,
A Division of Music Sales Corporation, New York, NY.

All rights reserved. No part of this book may be
reproduced in any form or by any electronic or mechanical means
including information storage and retrieval systems,
without permission in writing from the publisher
except by a reviewer who may quote brief passages in a review.

Order No. AM 37250
International Standard Book Number: 0.8256.2425.8

Exclusive Distributors:
Music Sales Corporation
257 Park Avenue South, New York, New York 10010 USA
Music Sales Limited
8/9 Frith Street, London W1V 5TZ England
Music Sales Pty. Limited
120 Rothschild Street, Rosebery, Sydney, NSW 2018, Australia

Printed in the United States of America by
Vicks Lithograph and Printing Corporation

Contents

Foreword

Considerable effort has gone into this volume to present the facts of music theory and basic playing techniques in the clearest, most interesting form, not making them rules or regulations to be strictly followed.

The author's success as an electric bassist represents his philosophy of sensitivity surrounded by talent, imagination and the basic foundation of the art of music.

Based on your attitude, enlightened self-interest, ability to develop yourself to your full potential, and your contribution to the well-being of music, you can promote your own success as an electric bassist. Your attitude represents the sum total of your thoughts and feelings. As a bassist, your success will equal your attitude.

Discipline and hard work, years of study, creativity and enthusiasm are as impressive as one's musical credits. Discipline is the self-gift of an extraordinary, gifted musician and is an attribute that makes the musical achievements possible.

ACKNOWLEDGEMENTS

JoAnn Jefferson, Bob Crenshaw, Jack Elliott, Alan Fergusen, Marina Easter, Whitman Mayo and Family, Pat Hicks, Bernard Purdie, The Family of James and Dorothy Thomas, George Bohannon.

MEMORANDUM

Walter Kerr, Ester Ports, Eloise Anderson.

Introduction

The Horizontal Electric Bass, commonly known as the Fender Bass (a brand name) is a newly created instrument in comparison to most other musical instruments. It has rapidly gained recognition for having produced the most exciting sound in today's music world.

Its success can be attributed to the changes in popular music during the time the electric bass was conceived. Music in the early fifties favored a melodic concept in which the bass was more felt than heard. The new music favored a rhythmic concept highlighting percussive, rhythmic bass tones.

Independent artists, orchestrators, band leaders and recording producers recognized this need and began utilizing individually styled electric bass players to fit their new production strategies, which proved highly successful.

When the instrument arrived on the market in 1951, it was described as a gimmick. It looked like a big guitar, but the sound resembled that of a loud upright bass. Its size allowed many musicians, especially guitar players, a chance to double without having to overcome the physical barriers the upright bass represented. Most of these musicians did not, and do not, master the instrument. They often confuse and misuse bass conceptions.

This does not mean that guitarists or horn players cannot or should not double on bass. The mere fact that the musician doubles on electric bass means that he or she is not a bass player first, but chose to play it as a second instrument. The player often does not have the training, conception, love or rapport of a player who chose it as a first instrument. Therefore, the music may suffer.

At the same time, a large number of upright bass players who have found a true rapport with upright bass playing approach the electric bass and find that the playing concepts are similar yet entirely different. However, their upright bass methods provide the ability to simulate electric bass playing well enough to "get by"; and again the music suffers.

There is also the problem that young electric bass enthusiasts encounter when they try to find a competent teacher. No other instrument of common usage has been so drastically neglected. The electric bass has come a long way since 1951, and in many instances has replaced the upright bass.

It is important that the electric bass and its concepts be studied. Equally important is a thorough understanding of the fundamentals of music. Music is an art. One must be well trained, interested and exist in an environment that complements natural ability. This text is designed to help beginning, intermediate and professional players with a basic step by step procedure in understanding how the electric bass functions in music.

The text is written from a right-handed point of view and is not meant to discourage or confuse left-handed enthusiasts by its terminology or procedures. A left-handed student can use this text by applying to it his or her own individual ingenuity.

The art of music is governed by the combined laws of harmony, theory and rhythm. These laws and theories must be studied in order to attain and maintain precious, unforeseen rewards that few musicians enjoy.

Using the Text

Information is systematically placed in the text to facilitate the instruction of any beginner, intermediate or semi-professional electric bassist or a student teaching himself. A teacher can pinpoint a student's needs and, depending on that student's level, use the text format and subject materials to expound on the fundamentals of music and the art of playing the electric bass. Each chapter's subject matter begins basically, broadens into an intermediate spectrum, and further broadens into the professional spectrum.

Four and eight measure duets are intermittently placed throughout each chapter for teacher/student interaction. Students teaching themselves will find adequate information and exercises to become proficient at reading music and playing the instrument.

The Table of Contents shows what and where the information is placed. Metronome settings should be selected by the instructor; the student without a teacher should select his own metronome settings for each exercise. Students should always begin slowly and graduate to quicker tempo settings.

Chapter One, pages 1-29, gives details on the instrument and its equipment, strings, fingers, hands, body amp, bar lines, measures and signs, staff lines and spaces, pitch, written range, sounding range (both clefs), right hand position/one finger technique, left hand position, tuning, tones/semitones and scales, and a fingerboard chart.

Chapter Two, pages 30-74, illustrates note and rest values and positions and fingering of major scales. The use of duets and note and rest values are outlined in a graduating sequence that further aids in reading music.

Chapter Three, Part One, pages 75-108, is a study of accidentals (flats). Exercises in the major keys of F, B♭, E♭, A♭, D♭, and G♭ are outlined. Each key appears in the order of its flat addition — fourths.

Chapter Three, Part Two, pages 109-151, is a study of accidentals (sharps) and uses the same format.

Chapter Four, pages 152-175, deals with the Natural Minor, Harmonic Minor and Melodic Minor scales and how they are relative and parallel in theory to major scales.

Chapter Five, pages 176-187, deals with augmented and diminished scales and takes a look at the tritone.

Musical term markings, dynamic expression of force, signs and abbreviated expressions, and accent marks, pages 188-189, end Book One.

Duets (Canons/Rounds) along with four and eight measure exercise duets are intermittently placed and graduate in complexity throughout each chapter. When using the duets to improve reading skills without an instructor, students should practice and record on a tape recorder the top line at a metronome setting of their choice, then practice the second line with the pre-recorded top line. The same format should be repeated beginning with the second part. Note: The metronome is very important, for it establishes and provides a consistent meter to practice by.

Chapter One

The Instrument and Its Equipment

There are many brands of electric basses on the market today. If you are not an experienced player, it will be confusing to you when you begin to look for an instrument and an amplifier. Ultimately, you will have to feel two things about your equipment. You must be comfortable with your instrument; it should not feel awkward to hold. You also need to have equipment that is suited to your style and the sounds you hear.

Of course, a beginner cannot be at ease with the instrument. It takes a few years to begin to develop a feeling for the subtleties of playing. For the beginner, an interest in complicated electronics and expensive equipment may be at the cost of his playing. You must practice, practice, practice. Only through playing will you develop your sound.

There is no single way to choose your first bass. Sometimes it is given to you, sometimes you buy the first one you see. The most expensive equipment is not necessarily the best. A bass can cost $29.95 and play like a dream. When you begin to hear the subtleties of sound, and the feel of the bass in your hands, you will automatically begin to experiment. But at first, play, play, play — and listen.

STRINGS

At present, there are three types of strings made for the electric bass. Strings vary in their basic composition (see below), scale and gauge. The scale you need is determined by the length of the neck of your bass. Most strings come in light, medium and heavy gauges. Your choice of gauge (or thickness) is dependent upon your touch, your strength, the size of your fingers, and the intangible quality of feel. These are things you will learn through playing.

Round Wound

The round wound string is the same kind of string used in the upright piano. Although the round wound string is not polished smooth, many professional players prefer it because it feels smoother to the hands than other strings. You may find more fret noises when you play a round wound string; however, fret noises are not always undesirable. An experienced player may also prefer the strong ringing tone and the greater variety of harmonics produced on a round wound. Remember that your choice of string will depend on the style of music you play, and your own sound.

Round Wound (Standard)

Consists of a steel string wrapped with a magnetically sensitive binding of nickel.

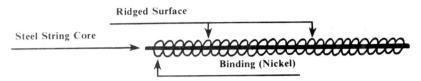

Flat Wound

The flat wound string is polished smooth, and does not give excess fret noise when played. This type of string is widely used on acoustic basses, and the acoustic bass player will generally use the flat wound string on his electric bass.

Flat Wound (Smooth)

Consists of a steel string wrapped with a magnetically sensitive flat ribbon of nickel or some comparable metal.

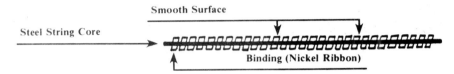

Nylon Flat Wound

Consists of a steel string wrapped with a specially formulated nylon ribbon.

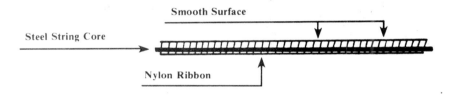

Two other types complete the basic analysis of **Electric Bass Strings**, they are:

Half Wound

A combination (50%) of round wound and flat wound.

Quarter Wound

Only one quarter of the overall string consistency is round wound. This string has a slightly smoother feel than flat wound.

Note: String makers produce different gauges of their strings, in order to provide a choice for each player's hand, finger size and personal preference. Also, the steel string core (center) of strings may be occasionally wrapped with silk.

FINGERS AND HANDS

You must learn to take care of your hands, for they are a vital part of your natural equipment. When you begin to play, or if you have not practiced for some time, you will find that your fingertips are sore. With practice, the soreness will disappear, and your fingertips will become calloused. You should not try to control the size and shape of your callouses, or the oil in your hands. Your callouses are your body's way of adapting to the instrument; they are as individual as your fingerprints or astrological chart.

Only by playing the instrument as much as possible will you learn how to use the unique properties of your fingers and hands to create your own bass tone. No one can teach you how your hands feel; that is why there can be no inflexible rules.

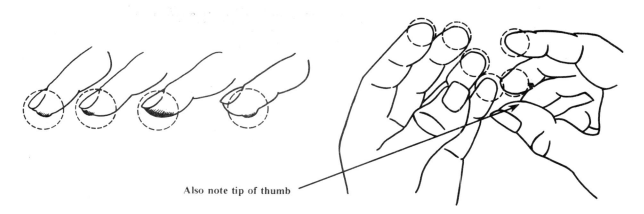

Also note tip of thumb

Every detail on your hand is unique. The size and strength of your fingernails are unique. Pay attention to them, because they are an important part of your right hand sound.

To shape your fingernails for playing the bass, begin by letting the nail grow to the tip of the fingers, or, if it is longer, cutting it back. This will give you an equal balance between the nail, which brings out the top (higher) end of your sound, and the pad tips of your fingers, which give you the mid-range and bottom. (Diagrams 1 and 2)

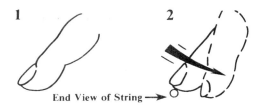

End View of String ➔

If you prefer more of a round, fat, heavy sound, just alter your attack on the strings so that you are applying more skin than nail. (Diagram 3)

Similiarly, if you prefer more of the top end in your sound, use more nail. (Diagram 4)

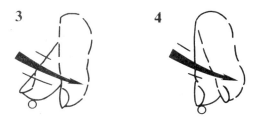

Sometimes you will need to push the limits of your endurance. If your muscles are tired or your fingers are sore, but you want to continue practicing, be careful that you don't unconsciously adopt poor playing habits from fatigue.

THE BODY AMP

If you sit correctly (placing your instrument on your thigh while the top of the bass rests on your chest), you can hear every note you play clearly. (Diagram 1)

Side View

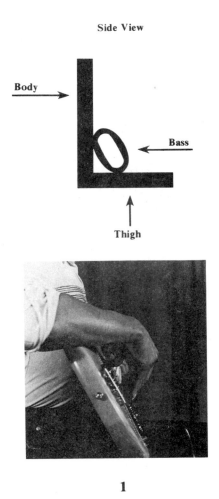

1

Standing, wearing the instrument across the *upper* body provides a clear sound and closer visual contact. Wearing the instrument below the hips or on the thigh limits playing ability. Beginners and other players uncomfortable wearing the instrument should try wearing the instrument across the *upper* body if not already doing so.

RIGHT HAND POSITION/ONE FINGER
PLAYING TECHNIQUE

This technique is a basic method that involves using one finger to play. Beginning pick-and-thumb players can, with an elementary approach, familiarize themselves with playing the instrument with the first finger. While playing and practicing, you must develop a mature stroke, pluck, pull, attack, or whatever you want to call the action you apply when playing on the strings of your bass. Your stroke must be mature — not haphazard.

Place the little, middle and ring fingers of the right hand on the pickup cover. This is the Position Bar. If your instrument has no pickup cover, modify the position to establish a consistent self-satisfying attitude for your touch and stroke. (See page 46 for examples of thumb positions and hand placement).

Position Bar

Place your thumb on the top of the E string (top string) with all of the natural pressure going into the bass and body. The idea is to merely rest the thumb on the string, not pushing down as you would to play a note, but making a sound hand position from which the finger can execute.

G String/First String (Bottom String)

The G string is physically the bottom string of the four strings on the electric bass and is the highest in pitch. Its placement on the neck, in the bass clef, on the piano keyboard and its octave notes are shown on page 23.

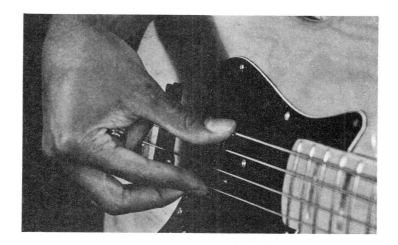

Move the *Position Bar* down toward the bottom of the pickup cover and place the tip of the forefinger on top of the G string. Keep the natural curvature of the forefinger and thumb, that create the *Position Bar*, locked in position while creating a slight tension between the thumb and forefinger: The spring that releases the tension is the muscle located in area A.

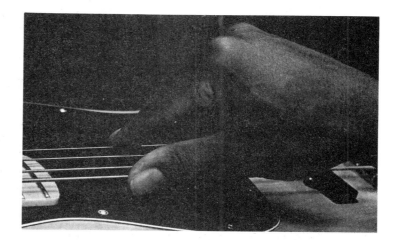

Direct any thumb pressure into the body of the bass, not *down* on the E string.

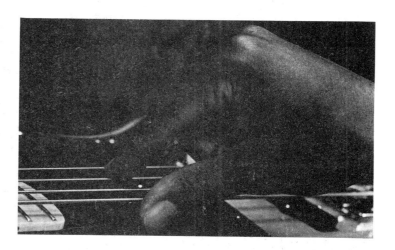

Release the imposed tension by snapping the forefinger into the string toward the thumb (like pinching the two fingers together).

D String/Second String

Its placement in the bass clef, on the piano keyboard and its octave notes are shown on page 22.

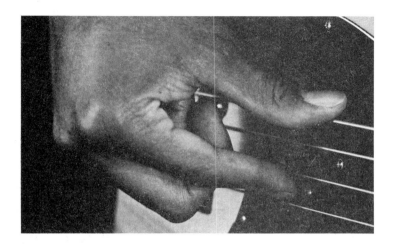

Maintaining the *Position Bar*, place the tip of the forefinger on the D string.

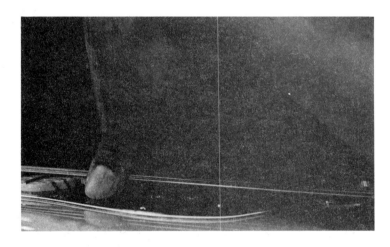

Maintain thumb pressure into the body of the bass.

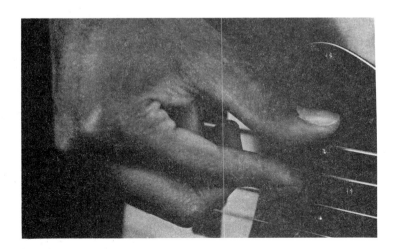

After Action

Snap forefinger into the A string toward the thumb.

A String/Third String

Its placement in the bass clef, on the piano keyboard and its octave notes are shown on page 21.

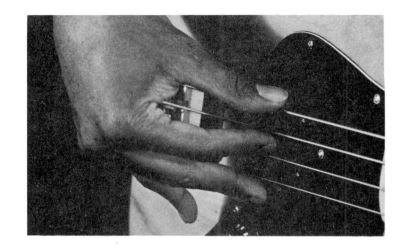

Adjust *Position Bar* to accommodate placement of fingertip on the A string.

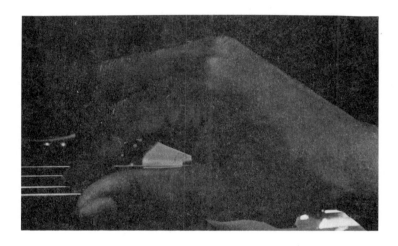

Maintain thumb pressure into the body of the bass.

After Action

Snap forefinger into the E string toward the thumb.

E String/Fourth String (Top String)

The E string is only physically the top string of the four strings on the electric bass; it is the lowest in pitch. Its placement in the bass clef, on the piano keyboard and its octave notes are shown on page 20.

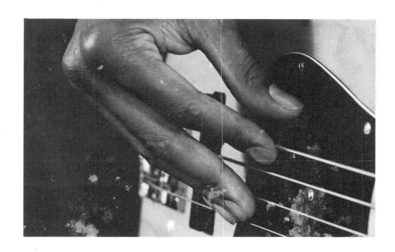

Adjust, as necessary, the Position Bar toward the top of the pickup cover. Move the thumb about one inch up, away from the E string maintaining the same pressure *into* the body of the bass.

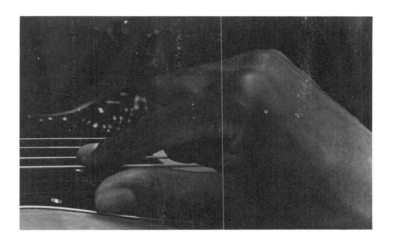

Most electric bass *pick guards* are different, so you must use your own discretion concerning thumb placement for playing on the E string. Try not to deface your instrument by gouging the wood in this area with your thumbnail.

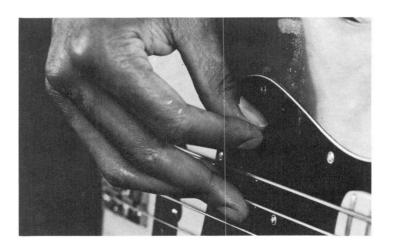

After Action

Snap the forefinger into the thumb.

*Pick guard— The instrument was originally designed to accommodate guitar players. The guard is a part of the style of the instrument and the design further protects the instrument from scratches and scars in that area from the use of a pick.

LEFT HAND POSITION

Although hand and finger positions may vary (depending upon style) when fretting notes to be played, one basic hand position for fingering notes on the fingerboard should be adopted. Placement of your fingers on the fingerboard (before, right after, or directly between the frets) is up to your own adaptation and judgment.

The frets are actually numbered and referred to in this manner.

Begin your study habits by playing directly between the frets, and thinking of the space between two frets as the actual playing area.

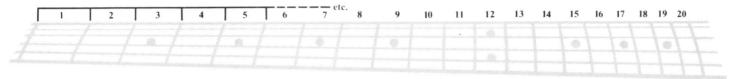

The thumb and middle finger provide the balance that permits the other fingers of that hand to function fluently. The thumb receives the weight of the neck and guides the fingers to playing position on the fingerboard.

Forearm, wrist and hand must work as one unit from the knuckles to the elbow. This will take time, like the hardening of the fingertips.

THE STAFF/LINES AND SPACES

The staff consists of five lines and four spaces that are labelled by using the first seven letters of the alphabet.

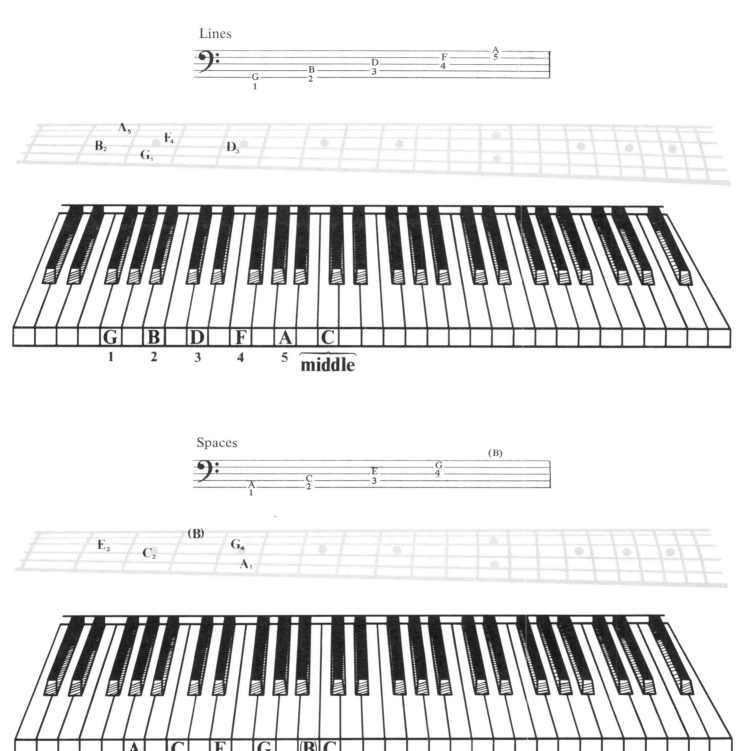

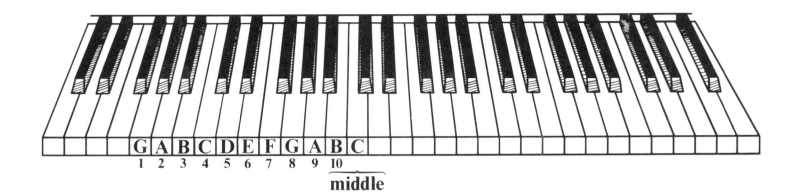

PITCH

Pitch is a term used to describe where a note sounds in the different clefs. To show the pitch of a note, clef signs are used at the beginning of staffs.

The *treble clef* (G clef) is ordinarily used to facilitate notes written above middle C.

The *bass clef* (F clef) facilitates notes written below middle C, an octave and a minor sixth down to E.

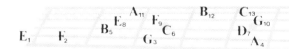

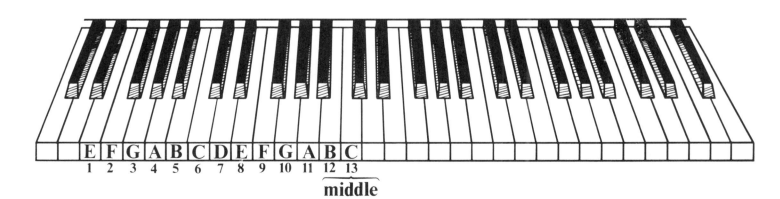

TUNING

The bass is the foundation of any musical unit. It is dominant, rhythmic and melodic at the same time. Constant tuning can be done skillfully while playing to insure that notes are being played in tune.

A low volume of the body amp will force you to pay more attention to your rapport with the instrument because you have to listen a little closer to what you are doing. This will help you to understand the differences in resonance that each string produces.

View the bass neck/fingerboard as though you were looking over the shoulder of your instructor.

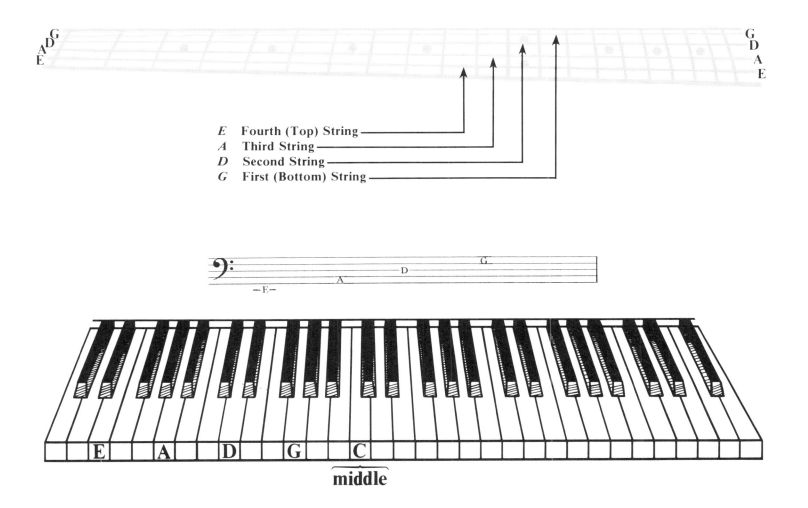

E   **Fourth (Top) String**
A   **Third String**
D   **Second String**
G   **First (Bottom) String**

OPEN STRING TUNING

A String

After tuning the E string from any given note, you can use the "Here Comes the Bride" method to tune the other three strings.

The first two notes of this popular wedding song are in fourths.

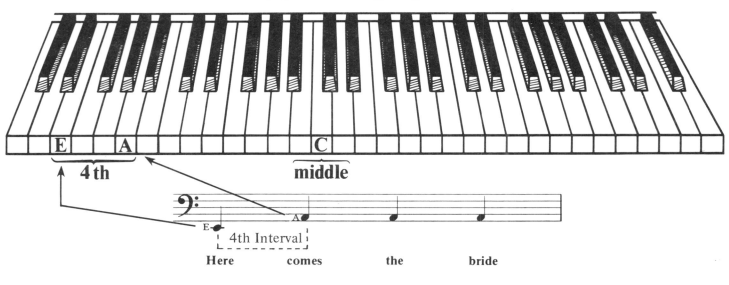

Here   comes   the   bride

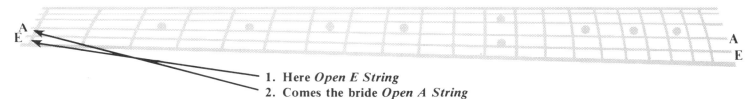

1. Here *Open E String*
2. Comes the bride *Open A String*

D String

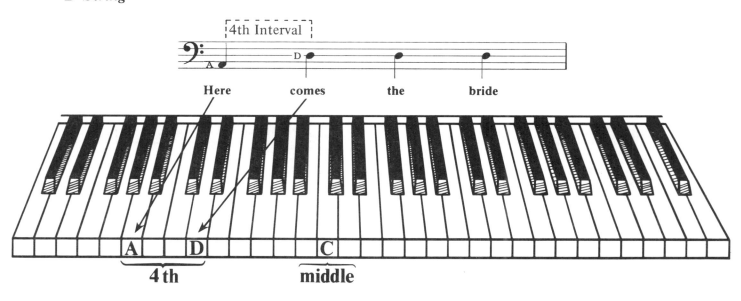

Here   comes   the   bride

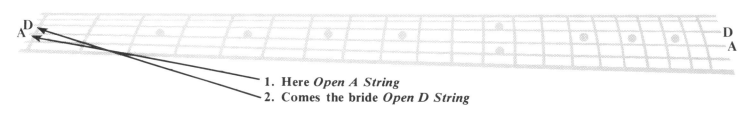

1. Here *Open A String*
2. Comes the bride *Open D String*

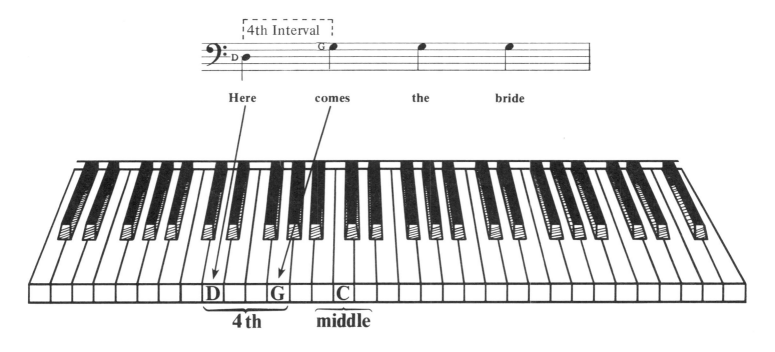

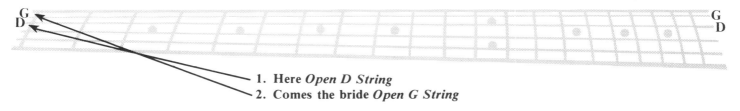

1. Here *Open D String*
2. Comes the bride *Open G String*

USING HARMONICS TO TUNE

A harmonic is an acoustical phenomenon produced by an altered touch to the string on the fingerboard. The harmonic represents the fundamental tone of the *OVERTONE SERIES. Once produced, its pitch and ability to ring serves as an excellent tuning device.

If you place (not completely fret) your forefinger lightly on the *A* fret of the *D* string (7th fret) and pluck the string, simultaneously lifting your forefinger, you can produce a ringing *A* harmonic that can be used to match the *A* of another instrument already in tune (the given note).

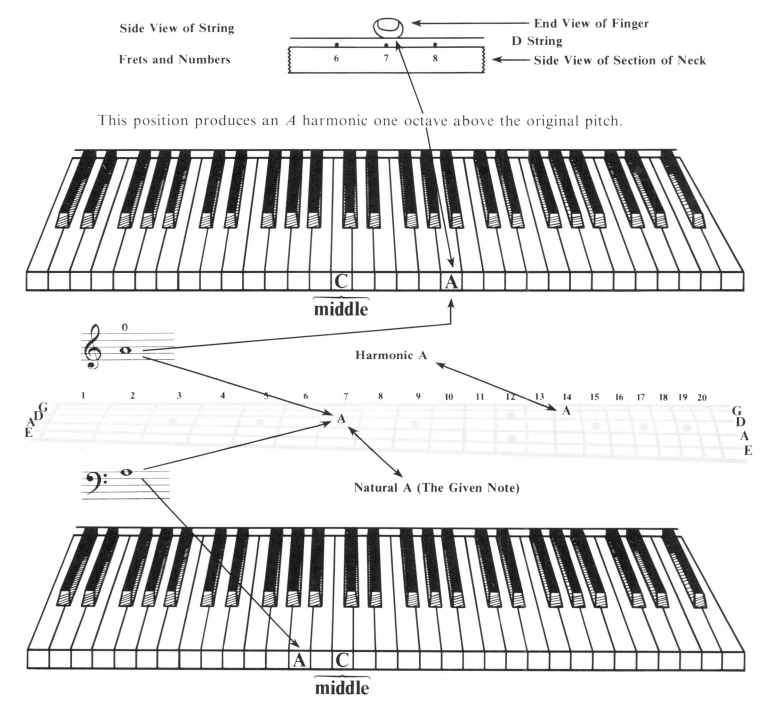

Side View of String — End View of Finger

D String

Frets and Numbers — Side View of Section of Neck

This position produces an *A* harmonic one octave above the original pitch.

Harmonic A

Natural A (The Given Note)

*OVERTONE SERIES: After producing any pitch, overtones and harmonics sound simultaneously with that pitch. Basically these tones are inaudible and depend a lot on the condition of the strings and the pickups.

G String

While the *A* harmonic note previously played is still ringing, completely fret and pluck the *A* on your *G* string (14th fret — Illus. 1) and tune it to the ringing harmonic *A* you previously played on your *D* string (Illus. 2). The two notes must sound like one note to be in tune.

Illus. 1   *Illus. 2*

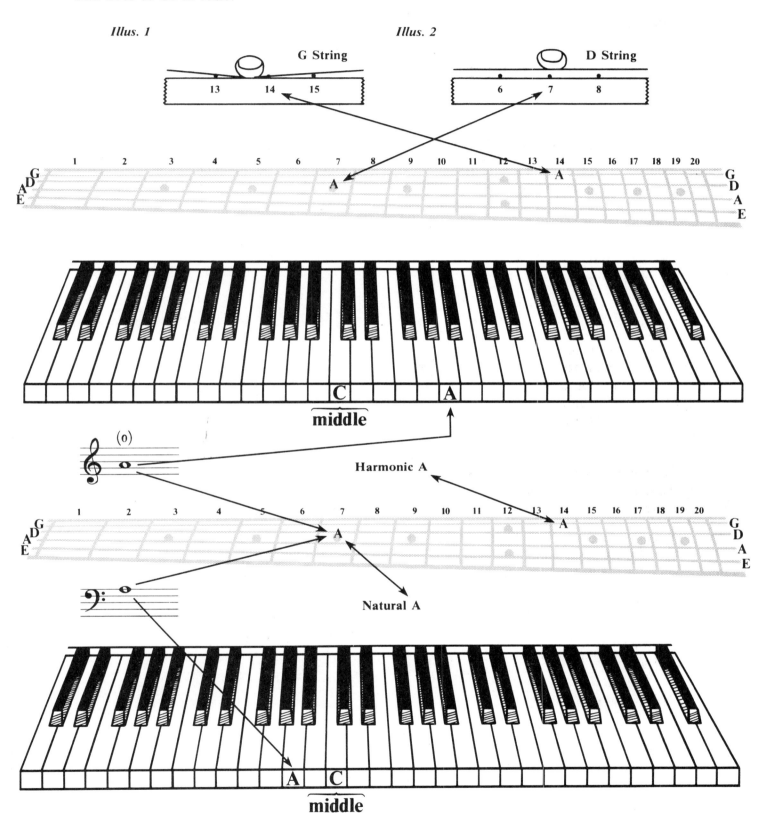

A String

Completely fret and pluck the *A* on your *G* string (14th fret — Illus. 3); then place (not completely fret) your forefinger on the octave *A* fret on your *A* string (12th fret — Illus. 4). Using both hands, simultaneously pluck the string with your playing finger and lift your forefinger from the fingerboard, producing an *A* harmonic note that can be raised or lowered to match the already tuned fretted note.

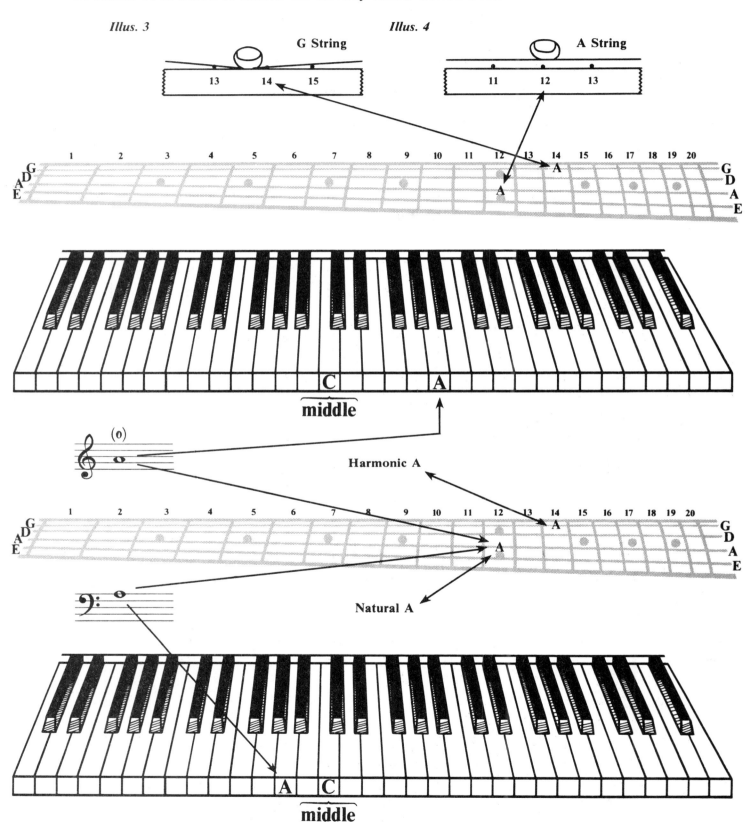

E String

The harmonic *A* on the *E* string can be difficult to hear because of its low resonance and condition of the bass, so I suggest, to properly tune the *E* string, just fret and pluck the *A* on your *D* string, then fret and pluck the *A* on your *E* string, and adjust the *A* on your *E* string to coincide with the already in-tune *A* on your *D* string.

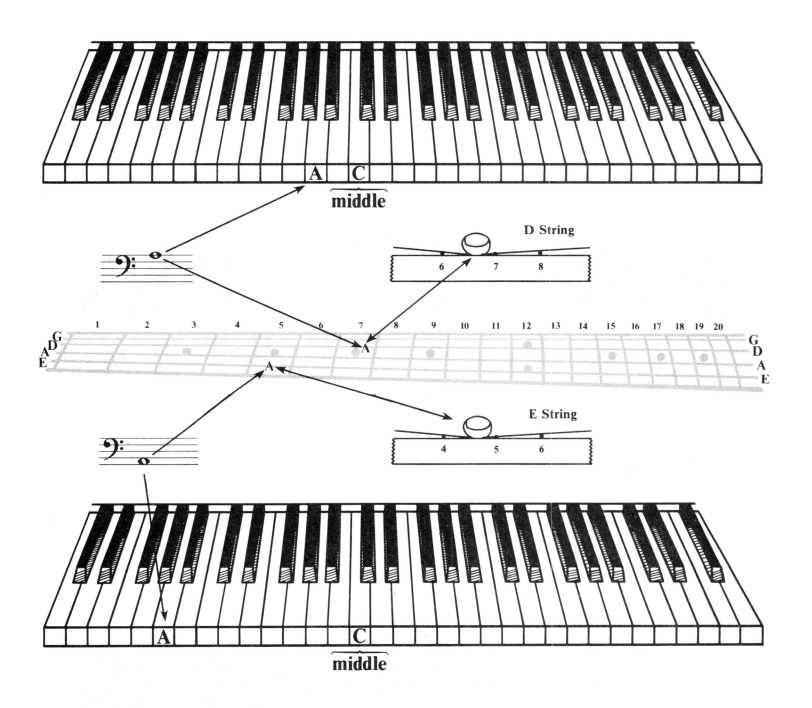

THE FINGERBOARD/OPEN STRINGS AND
THEIR FRETTED NOTES

E String and Notes

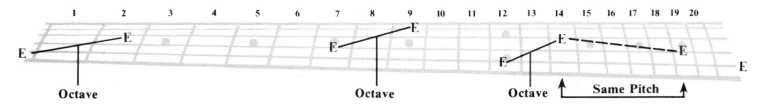

The diagram above shows the placement of the SEVEN E notes on the fingerboard of a twenty fret electric bass.

The diagram below shows the relationship and pitch placement of these seven notes to the *WRITTEN BASS CLEF* and piano keyboard.

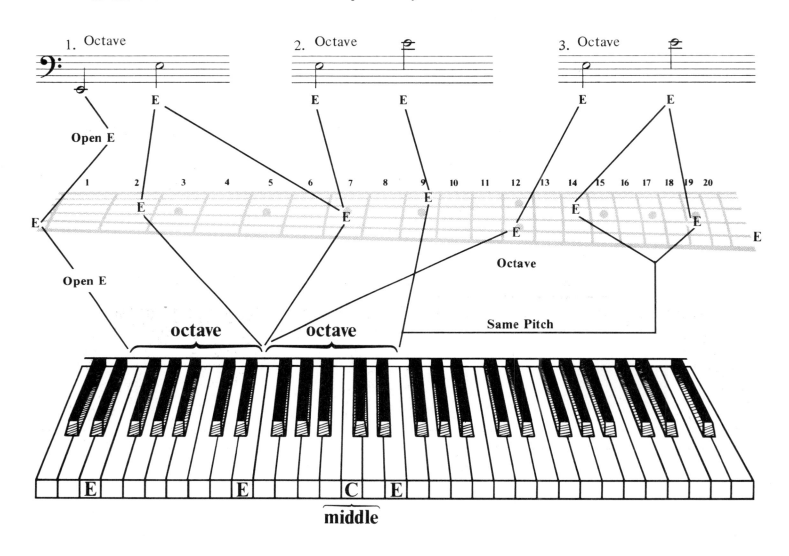

A String and Notes

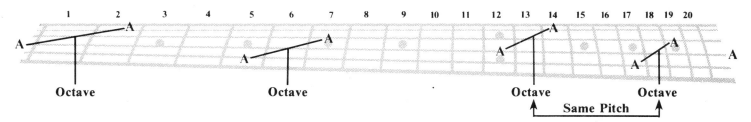

The diagram above shows the placement of the EIGHT A notes on the fingerboard of a twenty fret electric bass.

The diagram below shows the relationship and pitch placement of these eight notes to the *WRITTEN BASS CLEF* and piano keyboard.

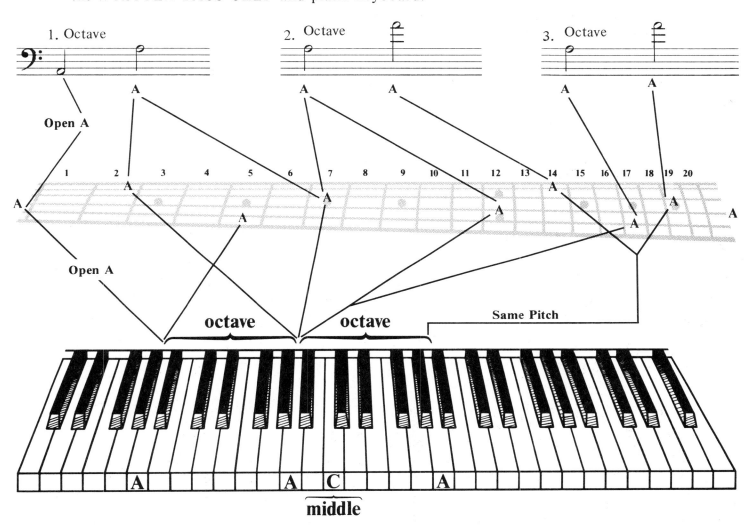

D String and Notes

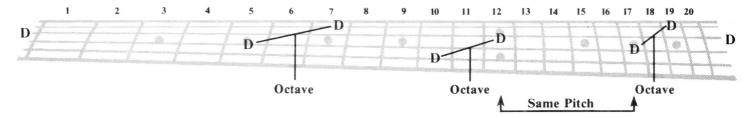

The diagram above shows the placement of the SEVEN D notes on the fingerboard of a twenty fret electric bass.

The diagram below shows the relationship and pitch placement of these seven notes to the *WRITTEN BASS CLEF* and piano keyboard.

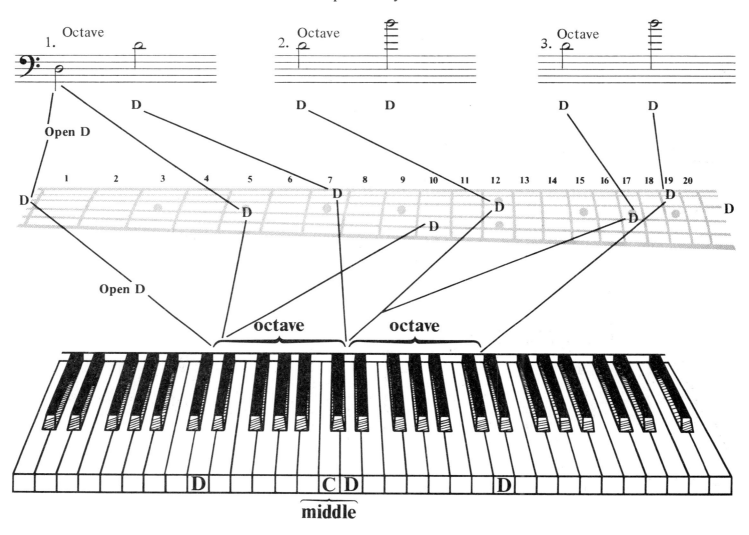

G String and Notes

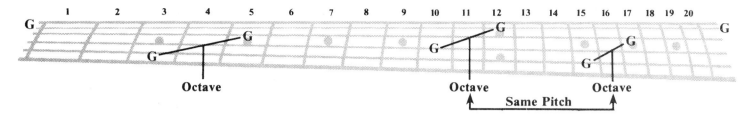

The diagram above shows the placement of the SEVEN G notes on the fingerboard of a twenty fret electric bass.

The diagram below shows the relationship and pitch placement of these seven notes to the *WRITTEN BASS CLEF* and piano keyboard.

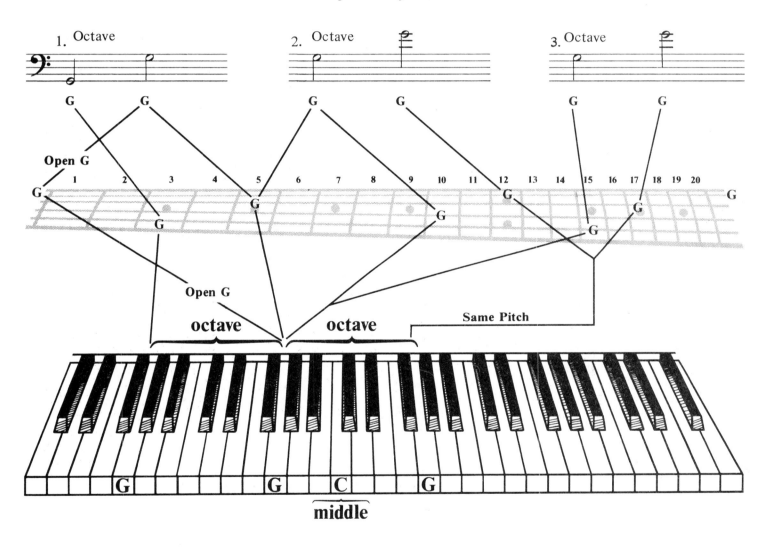

BAR LINES, MEASURES AND SIGNS

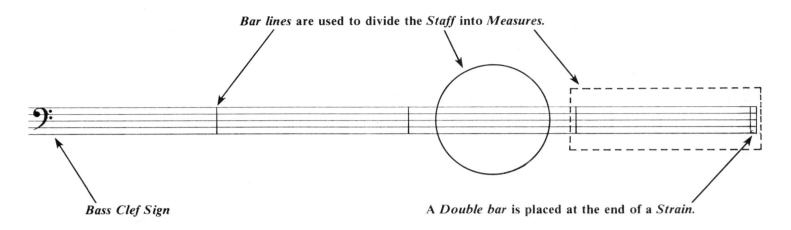

Bar lines are used to divide the *Staff* into *Measures.*

Bass Clef Sign

A *Double bar* is placed at the end of a *Strain.*

A strain is a complete musical statement ended by a double bar. Basically, in the music cultures of the western world, a strain is an even amount of measures, four, eight or sixteen in length.

A section of music that *repeats* is marked in the following ways:

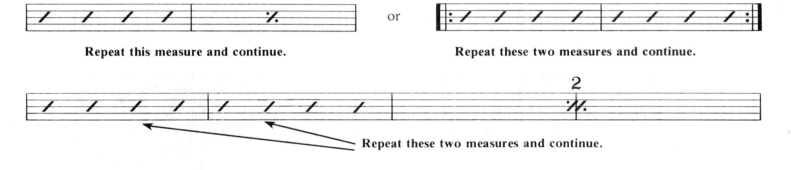

Repeat this measure and continue.

or

Repeat these two measures and continue.

Repeat these two measures and continue.

If a different ending is needed the second time a strain is played, a first and second ending are used.

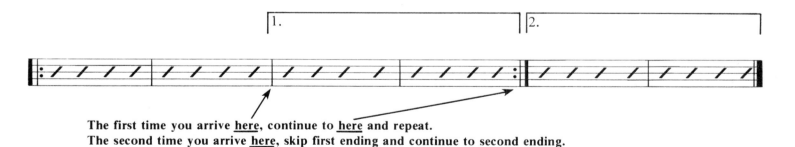

The first time you arrive <u>here</u>, continue to <u>here</u> and repeat.
The second time you arrive <u>here</u>, skip first ending and continue to second ending.

See page 188 for a continued explanation of music signs and abbreviations.

INSTRUMENT RANGE

There are makers who extend the range of the fingerboard by adding one to five more frets. All descriptions and diagrams relate to a twenty fret fingerboard.

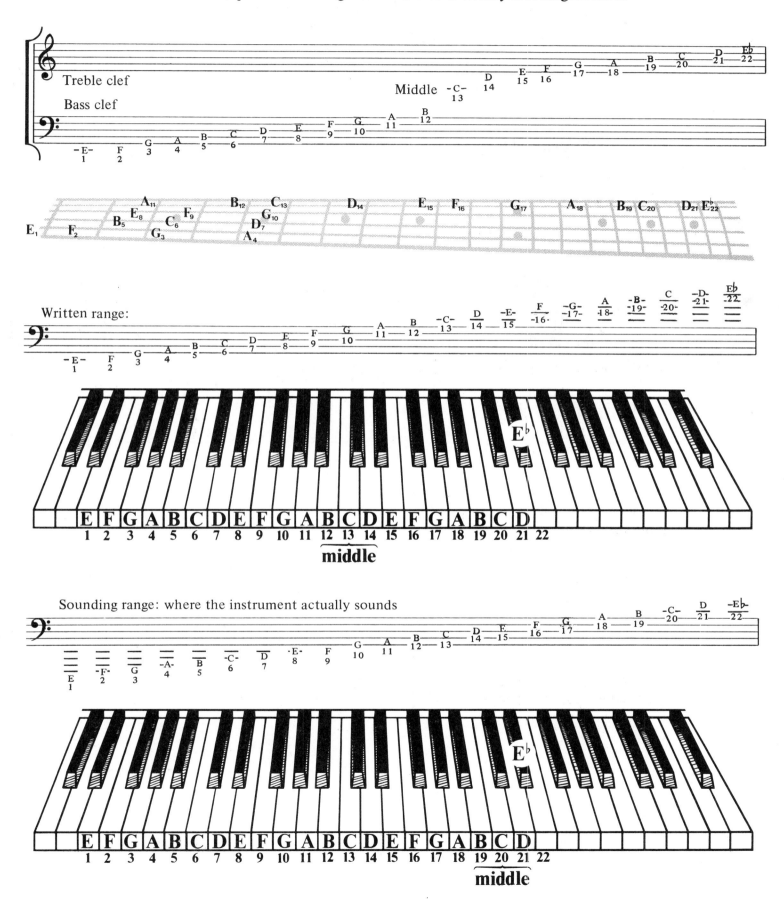

TONES, SEMITONES AND SCALES

Whole tones and *semitones* are *intervals* between successive notes and are sometimes referred to as *steps*. For example, the smallest interval used in the Western theory of music is the *semitone* (half tone/half step), occurring between the notes B and C and E and F.

A *tone* is equal to two *semitones*. Examples occur between C and D, D and E, F and G, G and A, and A and B. (Notice that by relating the written scale to the piano keyboard, a black key primarily divides each tone into two semitones.)

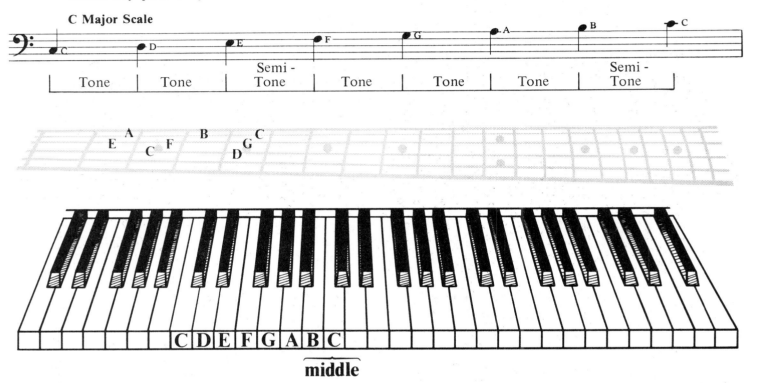

The C major scale establishes the pattern that all major scales will follow. The semitones occur between the third and fourth notes and between the seventh and eighth notes. All other intervals are tones.

A *scale* is best described as a series of notes that rise (ascend) and/or fall (descend) in pitch alphabetically, using any note and its octave (the eighth note above or below that has the same letter name).

Scales are *diatonic* or *chromatic*. The *diatonic scales* are classified major and minor and are a mixture of *tones* and *semitones*. (See scale of C major above.)

Chromatic scales move by *semitones* only.

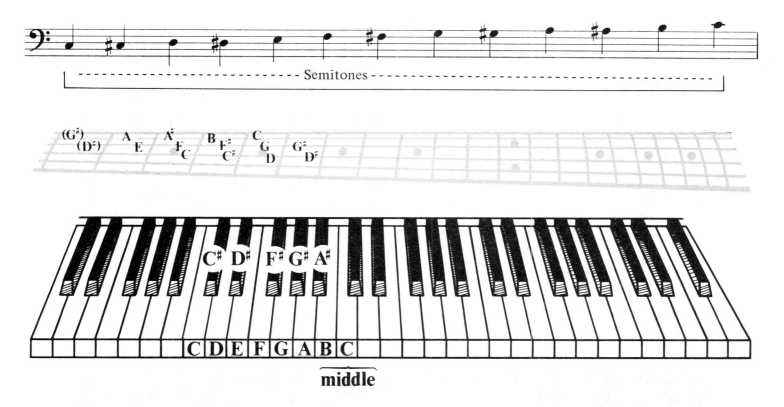

FINGERBOARD CHARTS/NATURAL NOTES

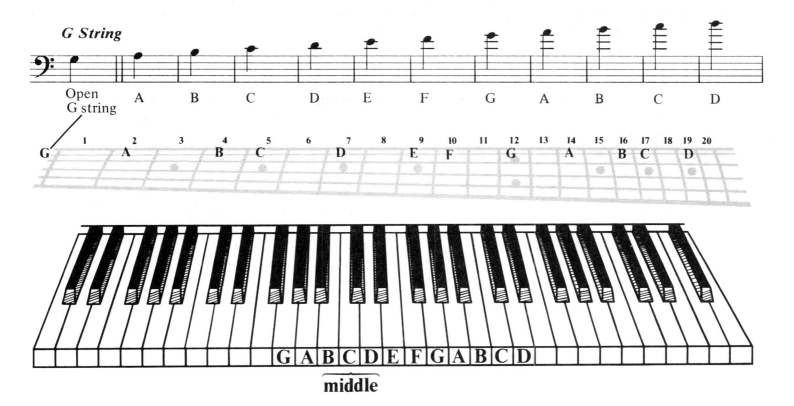

D String

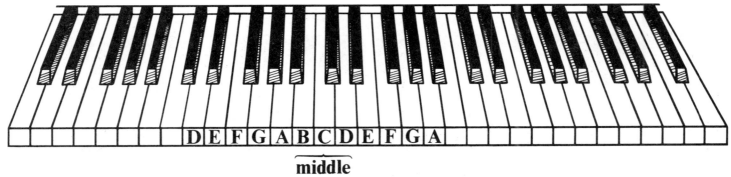

A String

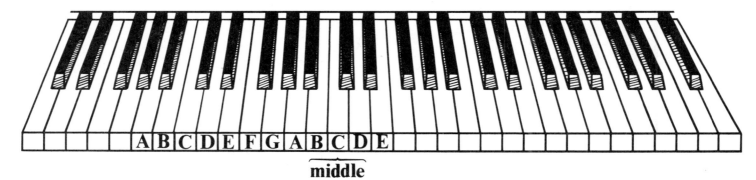

E String

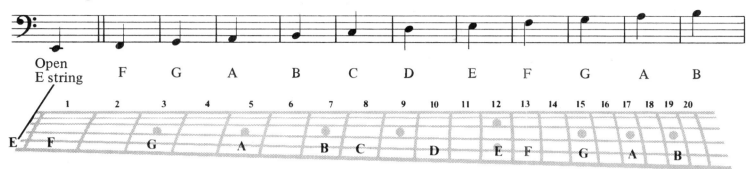

Open
E string | F | G | A | B | C | D | E | F | G | A | B

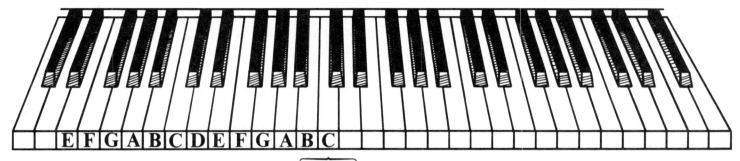

Chapter Two

Fingering Major Scales

The following chart and major scales show the relation of the written scales to the piano keyboard and the fingerboard of the electric bass. There are three basic ways to finger the major scales. To best facilitate a definite process by which you can begin playing these scales, we will use one basic method of fingering (with a few exceptions).

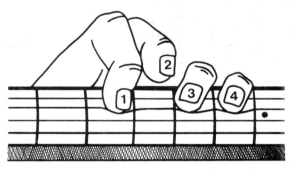

The playing fingers are numbered 1 through 4 consecutively.

The sequence of eight numbers (2 4 1 2 4 1 3 4) represents a practical and intelligent fingering procedure for playing the eight musical notes that comprise each major scale.

On the next page is a chart showing the C scale along with a piano keyboard, the neck of the bass and the sequence 2 4 1 2 4 1 3 4 for fingering. Every foot pat gets one note.

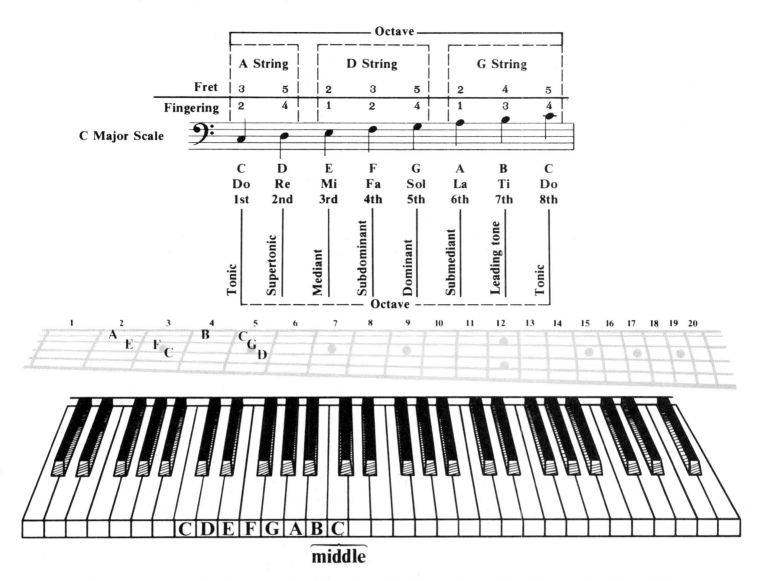

There are three basic areas on the neck of the bass where all scales can be played. One area you've seen in the preceding diagram. The diagram below shows another area beginning the scale on the E string (8th fret). The scale played here in the middle of the neck is in the same pitch as the preceding diagram.

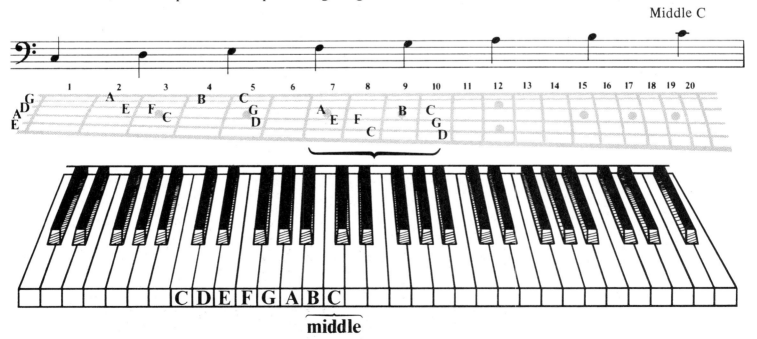

The third area begins the C scale on the A string (15th fret) an octave higher. The pitch is also an octave higher.

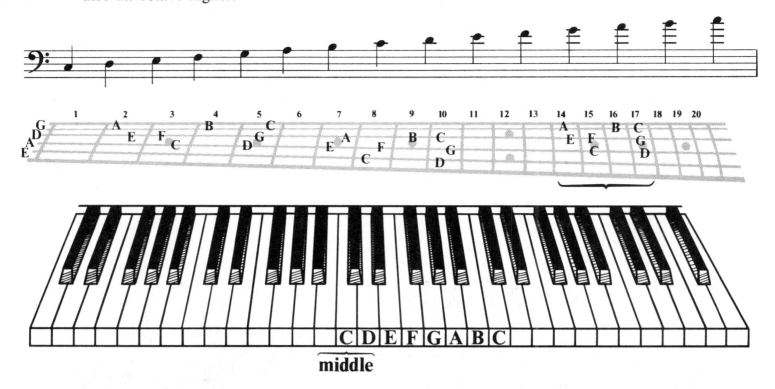

The fingering balance also changes to accommodate a natural and comfortable playing position for this area of the bass. The frets become closer to one another and your arm and hand are now in front of your body. This area is an octave higher than the two preceding areas. You can exaggerate the hand position and move the balance in your hand from thumb and middle finger to thumb and forefinger for comfort and logic.

After you have attained the ability to play the C scale in these three areas of the neck with accuracy, practice at different tempos with a metronome. This will help provide you with good timing, knowledge of the fingerboard, ear training, and set a premise for good chops (a term used professionally to describe endurance).

NOTE AND REST VALUES — C MAJOR SCALE

⑦ 2A 4A 1D 2D 4D 1G 3G 4G 4G 3G 1G 4D 2D 1D 4A 2A

⑧

2A 1A 4E 2E 1E 2E 4E 1A

⑨ 2A 1D 4A 2D 1D 4D 2D 1G 4D 3G 1G 4G 3G 4G 4G

4G 1G 3G 4D 1G 2D 4D 1D 2D 4A 1D 2A 4A 1A 2A

⑩

Eighth notes = one half of one beat per note (Part 1)

(Example 1)   (Example 2)

Beats: 1   and   2   and   3   and   4   and   1   and   2   and   3   and   4   and

Beats: 1   2   3   4

ARE YOU SLEEPING

*Canon/Round**

Francia Folk Song

*Canon — A melody is stated in one part, and is imitated for its entire length by another part. There are various types of canons, distinguished according to the distance of the parts (one, two, etc., measures). The most celebrated are the ten canons contained in Bach's "Goldberg Variations." A special canon used in popular folk music is also known as a "round" or a "catch". Examples include "Three Blind Mice," "Are You Sleeping," and "Row Row Row Your Boat."

TIED NOTES AND DOTTED NOTES

Notes are lengthened by ties or dots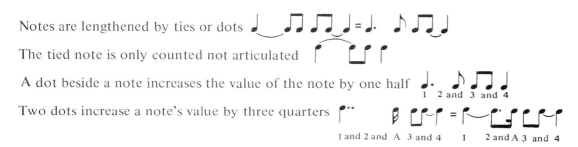

The tied note is only counted not articulated

A dot beside a note increases the value of the note by one half

Two dots increase a note's value by three quarters

STRENGTHENING THE LEFT HAND

Remember the left hand should be as secure and as independent as the right hand. You can strengthen your left hand by focusing your attention in that area and not using your right hand during the following therapy.

Using whole notes, half notes and quarter notes, play the C scale at a MM speed of 84 without using the right hand.

Do not force your fingers to play the notes at the same volume that two hands achieve. Tap your finger down on the note with a direct and normal motion, keeping that finger in place as you play the next note. This stretches the muscles in your hand from finger to finger as you move from note to note. Keep your thumb in place and maintain a good hand position. (See page 2-3).

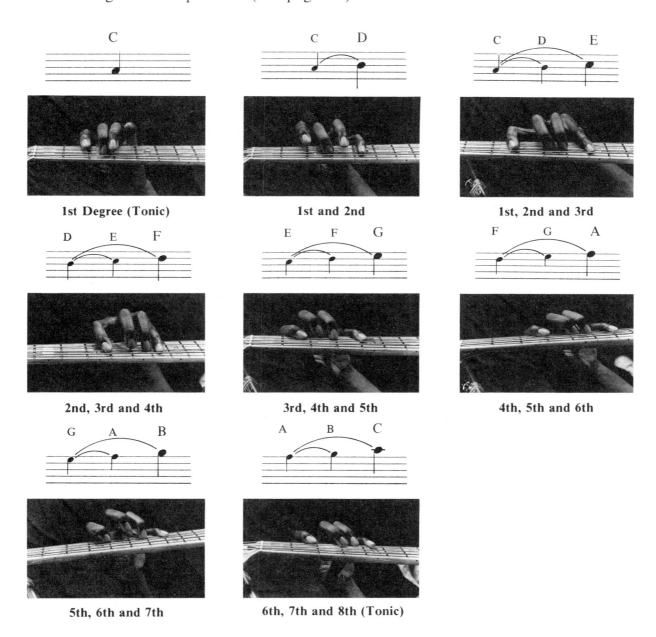

Rest when you feel the need. However, each day during study, work your left hand a little longer than the previous day, without the use of the right hand. This left hand therapy can be used as a warm-up session at the beginning of your study period. You can use this therapy on any exercise and all scales.

TWO FINGER PLAYING TECHNIQUE

It is absolutely necessary to establish a relationship between the fingers executing on the fingerboard and the fingers stroking, and strings. Over a period of time, through practice and actual playing, you will adopt attitudes and habits that are mental and physical. For instance, walking and running are *learned* functions which become involuntary. The mental and physical actions necessary to establish *your* individual ability in playing your instrument must also be practiced until, through repetition, they are also involuntary, or a natural function.

Up to this point in the text, one finger has been normally used while playing eighth notes, quarter notes and whole notes. When the tempo is faster, or when a more complex figure or *syncopation of notes are being played, it is necessary to use finger two (the middle finger) to physically help out.

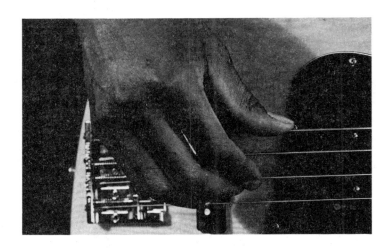

Hand Position

The sound produced in this area is a medium balance of a high and low tone. Moving the hand to the left towards the fingerboard produces a rounder sound and the strings are more flexible to the touch.

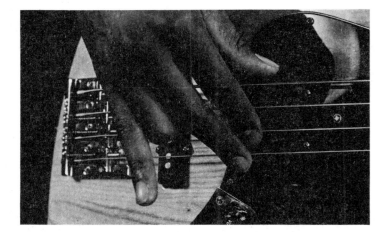

The sound produced in this area is higher tinted in sound. The further back toward the bridge you play the tauter the string is and the higher tinted the sound.

Your individual taste determines how many fingers you will use and what technique you will use to play different figures. The tips of each finger are physically designed by nature in different thicknesses. However, through practice (exercising) you can develop the same pads on each finger.

*SYNCOPATION: When the normal or expected pattern of rhythm or meter is deliberately upset by using a tie, dot, or accent mark.

G String/First String (Bottom String)

The two finger technique is approached in the same manner as the one finger technique (page 5), the only difference being there is basically no *Position Bar*. However, the imaginary spring located between the thumb and the forefinger is now extended to finger two.

Step 1: Before Action

The playing action of the forefinger (first finger) is described on page 5. Note the same spring area in playing action.

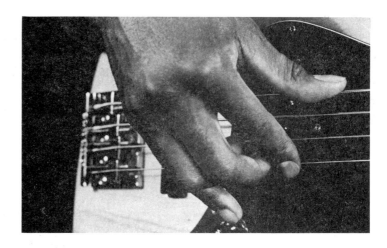

Step 2: After Action

Snap finger one towards thumb.

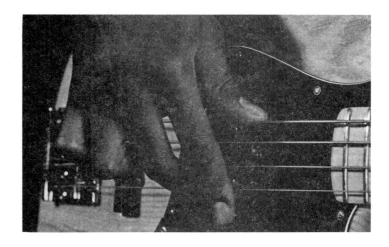

Step 3: After Action, Second Finger

After executing with finger one, follow with finger two, maintaining a sturdy and practical hand position. Utilize the information on page 32 in finding and arriving at a comfortable hand position.

D String/Second String

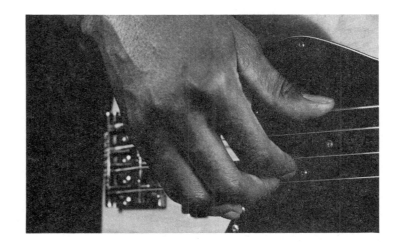

Step 1

The pinch is a bit smaller, so adjust.

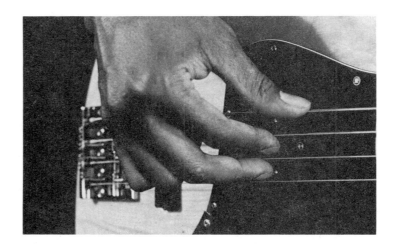

Step 2

Snap finger one into the A string towards the thumb.

Note: After acting with finger one, it is up to your judgment (depending on the music) whether to leave the finger on the A string or raise it out of the way as shown in step 3.

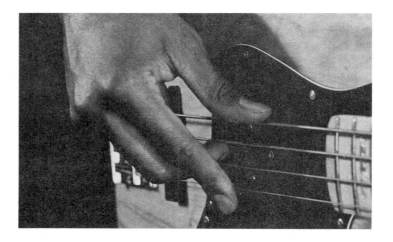

Step 3

Repeat step 2 with finger two.

A String/Third String

Step 1

The pinch here is smaller yet.

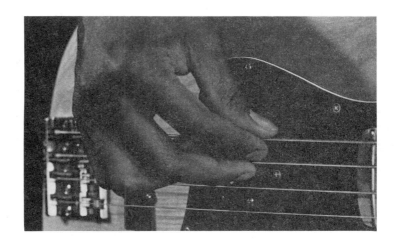

Step 2

Snap finger one into the E string and the thumb.

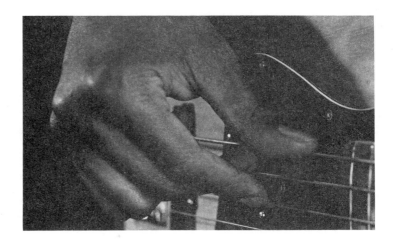

Step 3

Repeat step 2 with finger two.

Note: For stability, you can employ a Position Bar* (if you are using a pickup cover) by using the last two fingers of the hand.

*Position Bar, see page 5.

E String/Fourth String (Top String)

Again, the E string is only physically referred to as the top string of the four strings on the electric bass. It is the lowest in pitch.

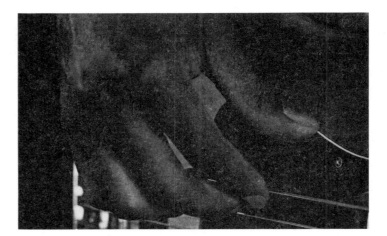

Step 1

Adjust the hand as necessary to facilitate the first finger's stroke (snap).

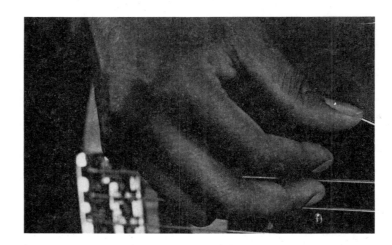

Step 2

Snap finger one into the thumb. Again, do not deface the instrument by digging out the wood with your thumbnail in this area.

Step 3

Repeat step 2 with finger two. Here again, if you are using a pickup cover, you might employ a Position Bar (3rd and 4th fingers) to maintain a sound hand position.

Practice these exercises alternating fingers one and two until you feel safe and secure in evenness. Note: Make the metronome setting of 118 the basic goal.

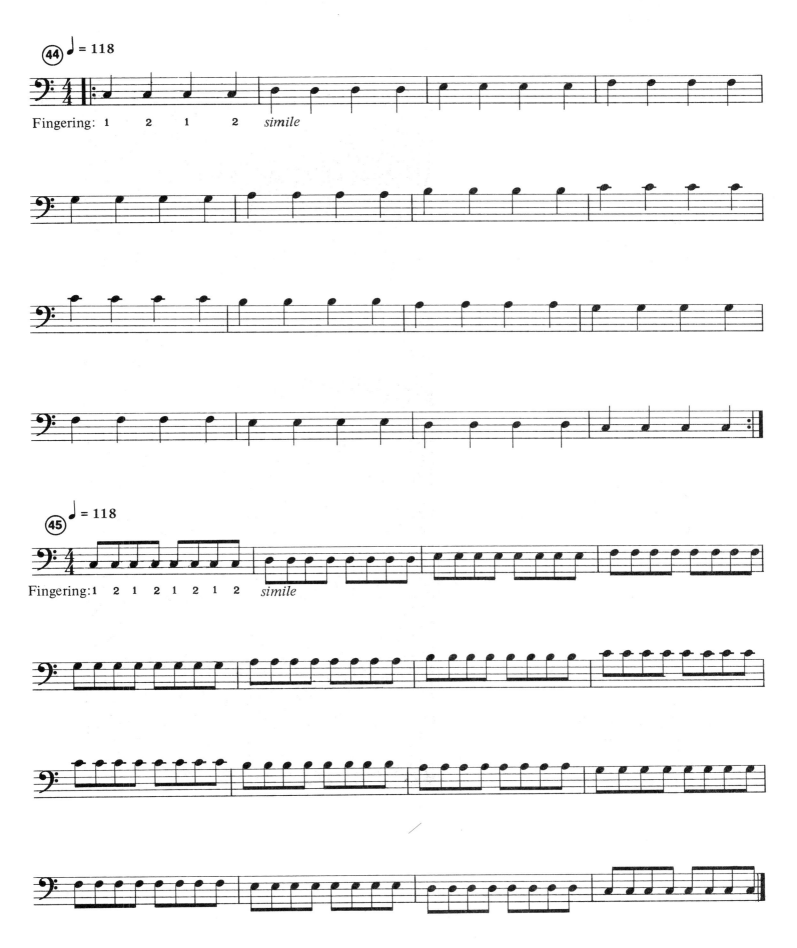

Practice the following four bar pattern alternating fingers one and two as shown.

A little different for dexterity and touch.

Practice, using your own discretion as to which fingers to use.

This exercise further aids the ability to use two fingers for cross-string dexterity. Use your own pace and ability during study.

Use your imagination and invent your own exercises to develop the muscles of both hands. Muscle strength here is necessary and promotes the endurance and ability necessary in using the two finger style.

TRIPLETS

The triplet feeling concept can be described like that of a waltz. Although a waltz is written in 3/4 time, the study below written in 4/4 has the same triplet feeling and can be attained in concept if you understand how a waltz is written and what a waltz feels like.

Each beat receives three evenly distributed notes. Mentally accent the first beat of each triplet.

THREE AGAINST ONE

Put a mental emphasis on each downbeat in order to insure a steady meter/time from triplet to triplet.

The eighth rest is a silent count that has the same value as the eighth note that it replaces.

Compound Triplets (Quarter Note Triplets)

The term "compound" refers to a triplet feeling which utilizes the quarter note feeling of three against two; three notes played against two beats in even succession.

Six quarter notes gathered (compounded) evenly in groups of three (triplets) are expounded against four quarter beats.

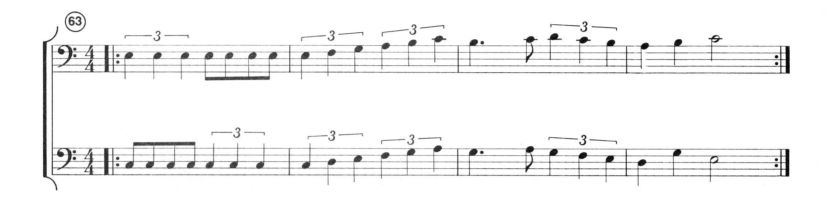

Half Note Triplets
Three notes played evenly against four beats (See No. 64).

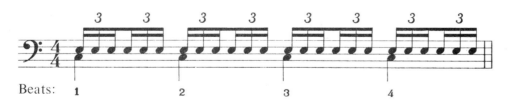

Sixteenth Note Triplets
Three notes downbeat plus three notes upbeat played against one beat (See No. 68).

Compound Sixteenth Note Triplets
Six notes played evenly against one beat (See No. 68).

Basic Triplet Description

Beats: **1**   **2**   **3**   **4**

Triplet Example 1

Beats: **1**   **2**   **3**   **4**

—59—

ROW ROW ROW YOUR BOAT

Canon/Round

Folk Song

Basic Triplet Description

Beats: 1   2   3   4

Triplet Example 2

Beats: 1   2   3   4

Player 1 reads and repeats the top line of this eight measure exercise once (sixteen measures) and continues on to the bottom line after the second repeat.

Player 2 reads and repeats the bottom line of this eight measure exercise once (sixteen measures) and continues on to the top line after the second repeat.

Example 3. Although the dotted eighth note and sixteenth note notation is not a triplet, its shuffle* feeling is directly related to the triplet feeling.

Basic Triplet Description

*Shuffle: See Book 2

SIXTEENTH NOTES AND SIXTEENTH RESTS (PART 1)

Sixteenth notes = four notes per beat

Sixteen rest = one fourth of one beat
four sixteenth rests = quarter rest

1 E and A 2 E and A 3 E and A 4 E and A   1/4 1/4 1/4 1/4   1/4 1/4 1/4 1/4

(84)

Beats: 1   2   3   4

SIXTEENTH NOTES (PART 2)

Syncopation can be read with security by relating to and recognizing on sight five main sixteenth note groupings. We have studied four and they are shown below with the fifth. Notice the physical character of the downbeat in each group and relate it to the mental count of that figure.

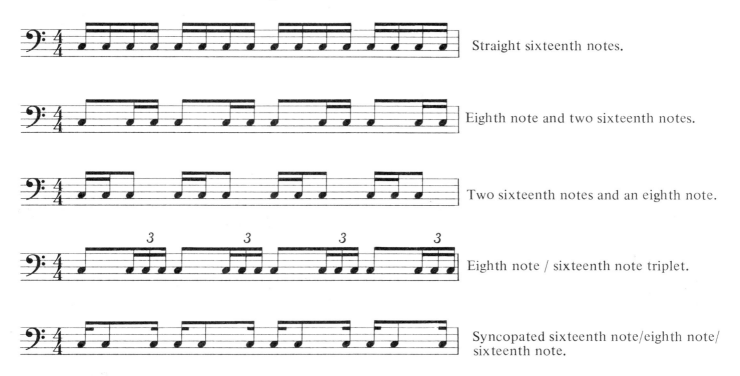

Straight sixteenth notes.

Eighth note and two sixteenth notes.

Two sixteenth notes and an eighth note.

Eighth note / sixteenth note triplet.

Syncopated sixteenth note/eighth note/ sixteenth note.

The following exercises within the C scale were created for studying syncopation. Knowledge and memory of the C major scale at this point will help in practicing syncopation and developing your ear training.

Chapter Three

Accidentals

PART 1: FLATS

A *flat* sign ♭ placed before a note *lowers* that note a half tone in pitch.

The note *B* is now flatted by a half tone. Note: B♭ and A♯ are fingered in the same way.

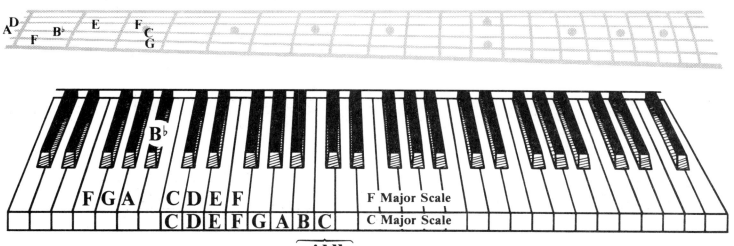

A *double flat* sign 𝄫 lowers a note one whole tone. This occurs when altering a note that adheres to a strict harmonic structure of the intended chord.

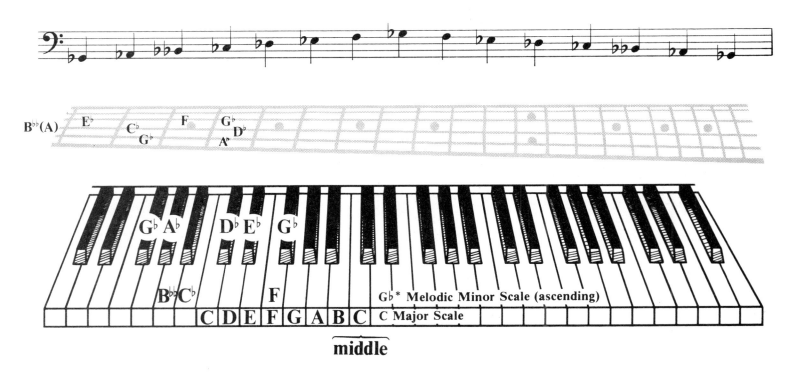

A *natural* sign ♮ placed before a note restores that note to its original pitch.

The note C (descending) is restored to its natural pitch.

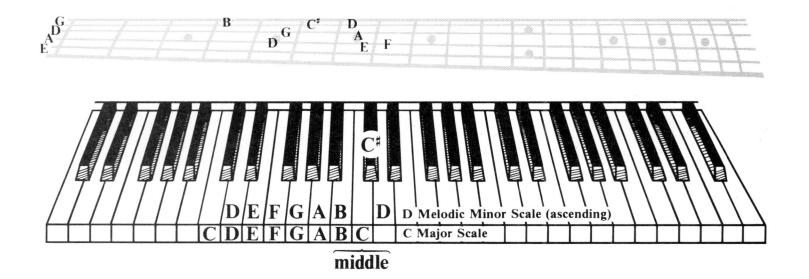

*Melodic Minor Scale, see page 159.

KEY SIGNATURE (PART 1) FLATS

To avoid writing a lot of accidentals, the necessary flats and sharps are grouped and written at the beginning of the staff, following the clef sign:

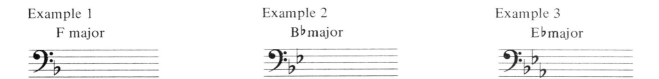

Example 1
F major

Example 2
B♭major

Example 3
E♭major

These are called key signatures, and govern the notes that follow throughout the music. The music will be in a definite key, named after the scale that is in use.

Example 1 shows the key of F major. The key of F uses the F major scale and requires that the note B be flatted.

F Major Scale

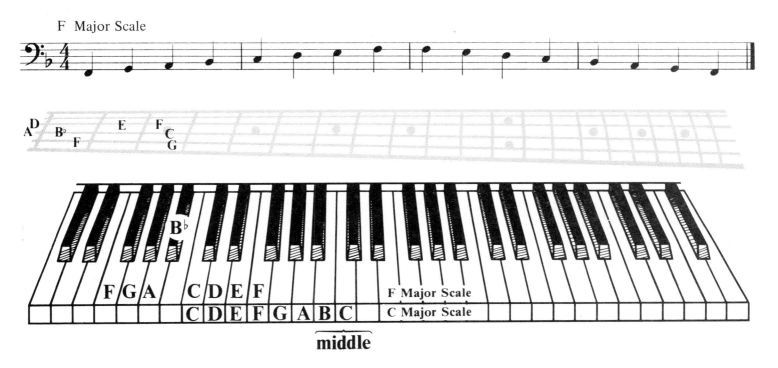

Every B note throughout the music is to be flatted (unless contradicted by another accidental).

Example 2 shows the key of B♭ major that flats the notes B and E.

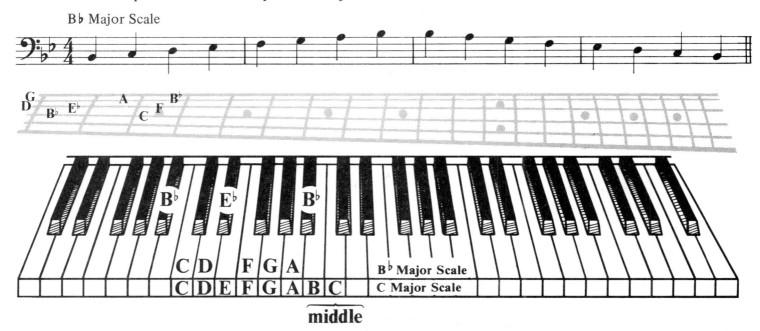

Every B and E note throughout the music is to be flatted (unless contradicted by another accidental).

Example 3 shows the key of E♭ major that flats the notes A, B, and E.

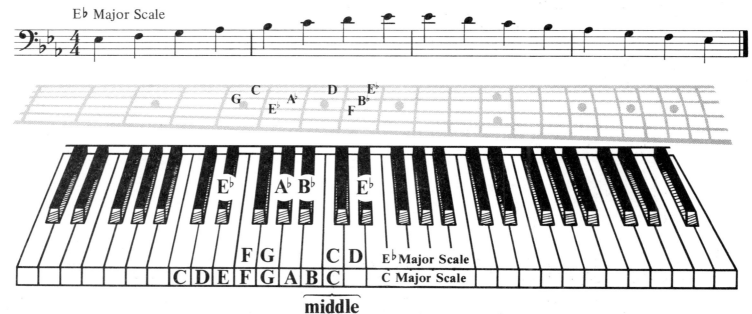

Every B, E, and A note throughout the music is to be flatted (unless contradicted by another accidental).

FINGERBOARD CHARTS/FLATS

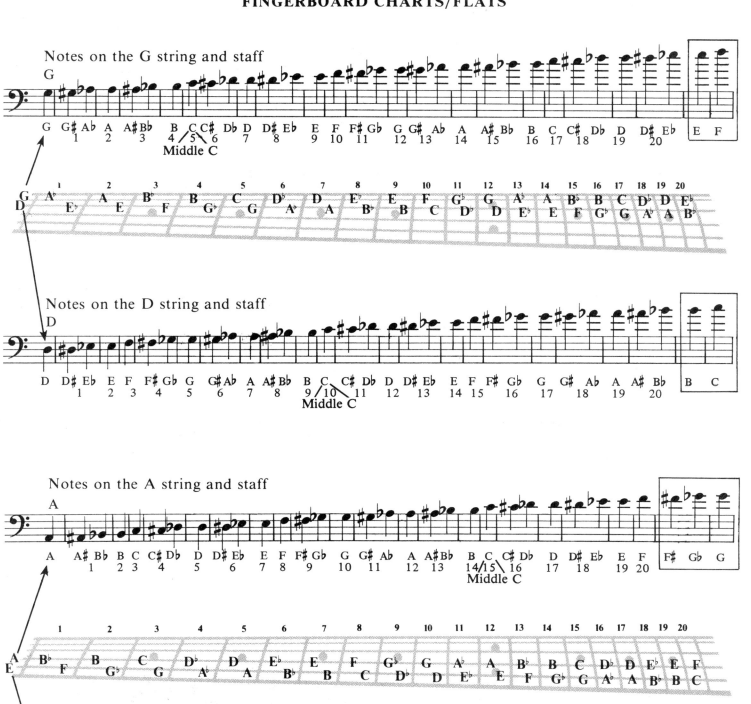

F MAJOR SCALE

1 and 2 and 3 and 4 and   1 and 2 and 3   4 and 1   2 and 3   4   1   2 and 3   4

Extended range exercise in the key of F — Using another position on the fingerboard.

2A   4A   1D   2D   4D   1G   3G   4G   4G   3G   1G   4D   2D   1D   4A   2A

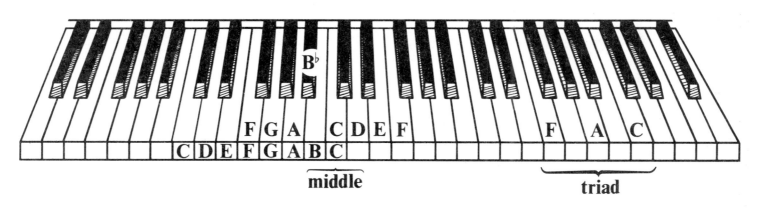

B FLAT MAJOR SCALE

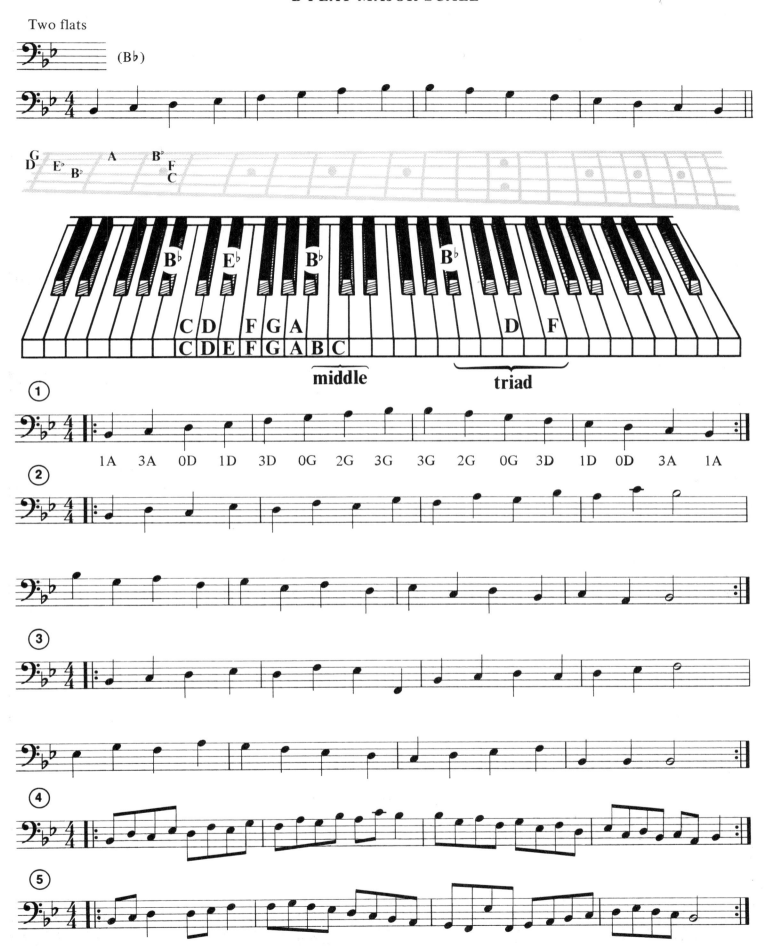

Extended range exercise in the key of B♭ — Using another position on the fingerboard.

3G 4A 1E   4G 1D   4G   4G 1D 2E

E FLAT MAJOR SCALE

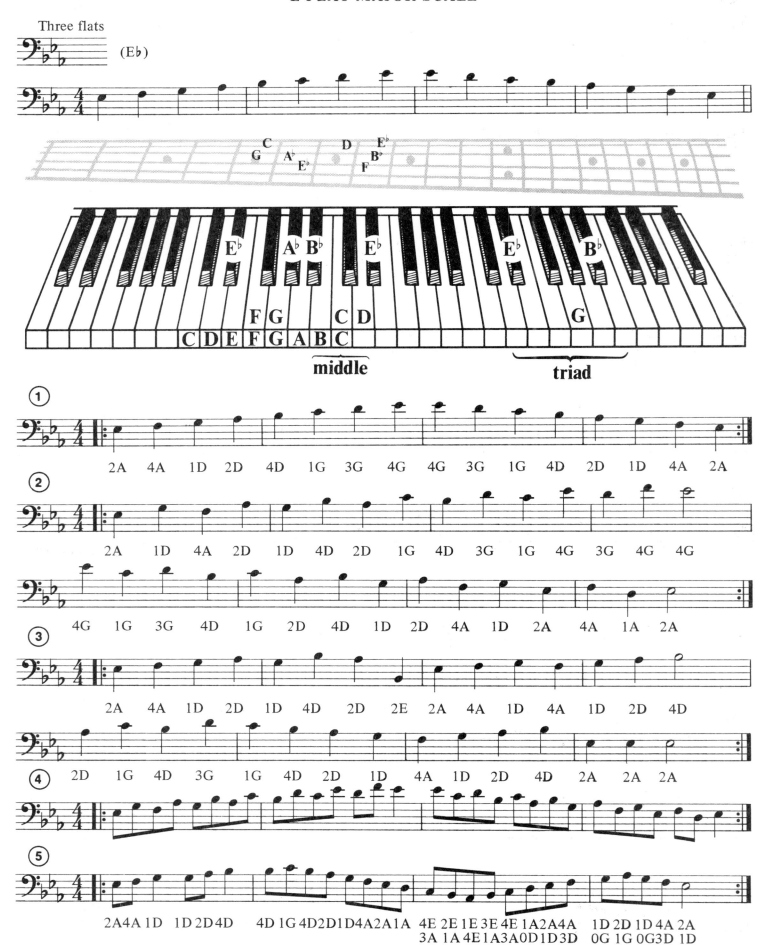

A FLAT MAJOR SCALE

D FLAT MAJOR SCALE

PART 2: SHARPS

A *sharp* sign ♯ placed before a note *raises* that note a half tone in pitch.

The note *F* is now sharped a half tone. Note: F♯ and G♭ are fingered in the same way.

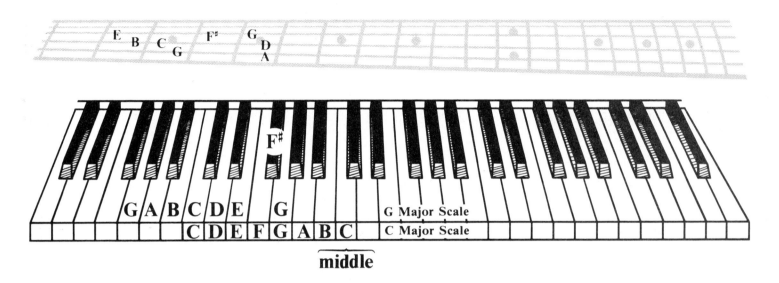

A *double sharp* sign ✕ placed before a note raises that note one whole tone. This occurs when altering a note that adheres to a strict harmonic structure of the intended chord.

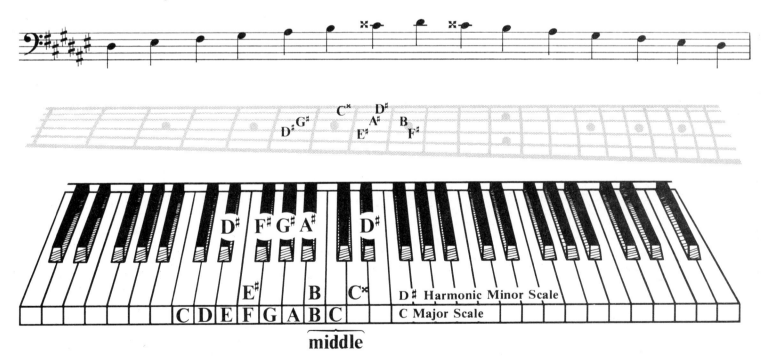

The D♯ Harmonic Minor Scale: This scale*, enharmonically spelled, is the same scale as the E♭ Harmonic Minor Scale (See page 156).

*Enharmonic, see pages 176-177.

KEY SIGNATURE (PART 2) SHARPS

To avoid writing a lot of accidentals, the necessary sharps and flats are grouped and written at the beginning of the staff, following the clef sign:

These are called key signatures, and govern the notes that follow throughout the music. The music will be in a definite key, named after the scale that is in use.

Example 1 shows the key of G major. The key of G uses the G major scale and requires that the note F be sharped.

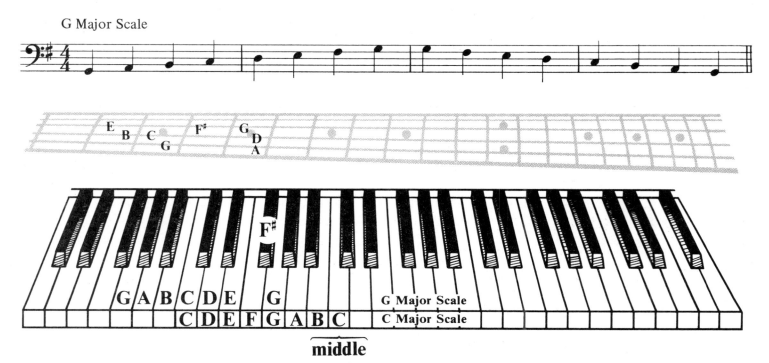

Every F note throughout the music is to be sharped (unless contradicted by another accidental).

Example 2 shows the key of D major that sharps the notes F and C.

D Major Scale

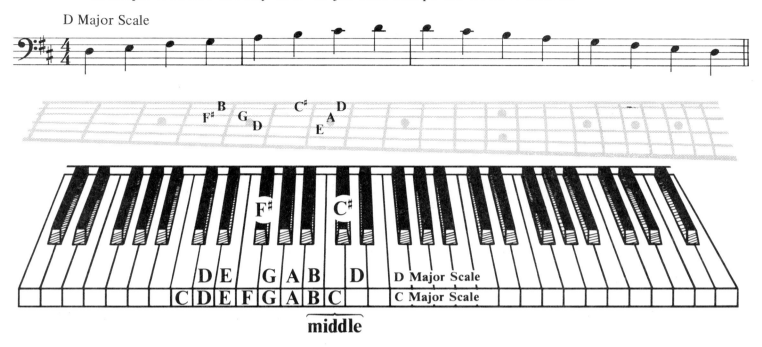

Every F and C note throughout the music is to be sharped (unless contradicted by another accidental).

Example 3 shows the key of A major that sharps the notes F, C, and G.

A Major Scale

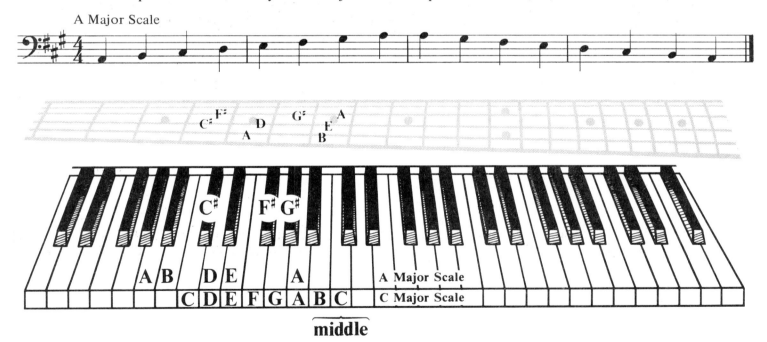

Every F, C, and G note throughout the music is to be sharped (unless contradicted by another accidental).

FINGERBOARD CHARTS/SHARPS

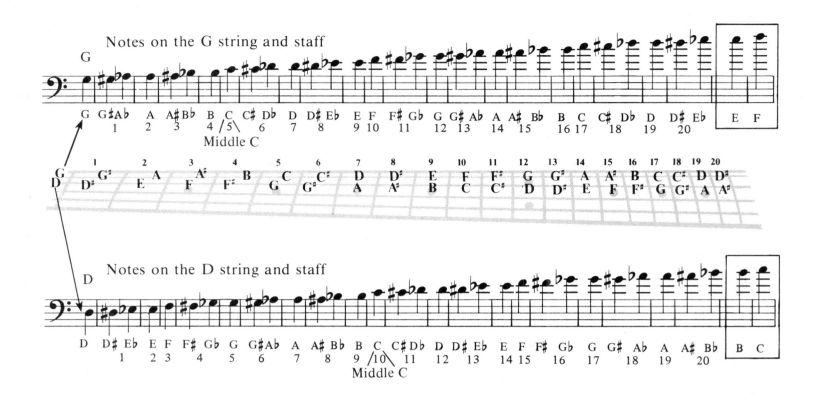

Notes on the G string and staff

Notes on the D string and staff

Notes on the A string and staff

Notes on the E string and staff

G MAJOR SCALE

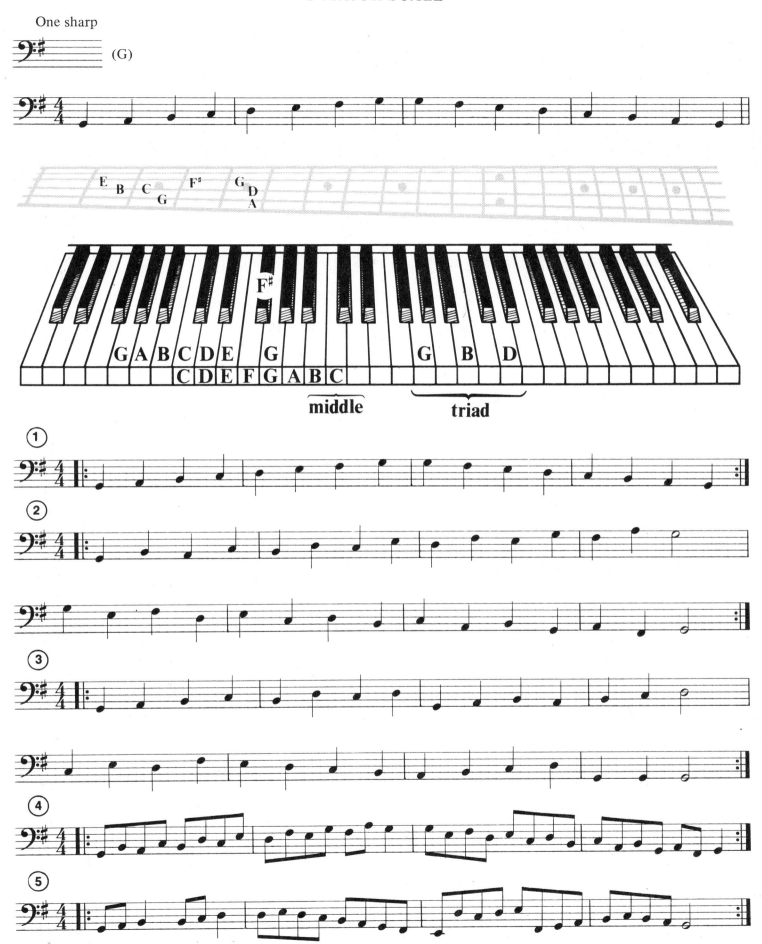

D MAJOR SCALE

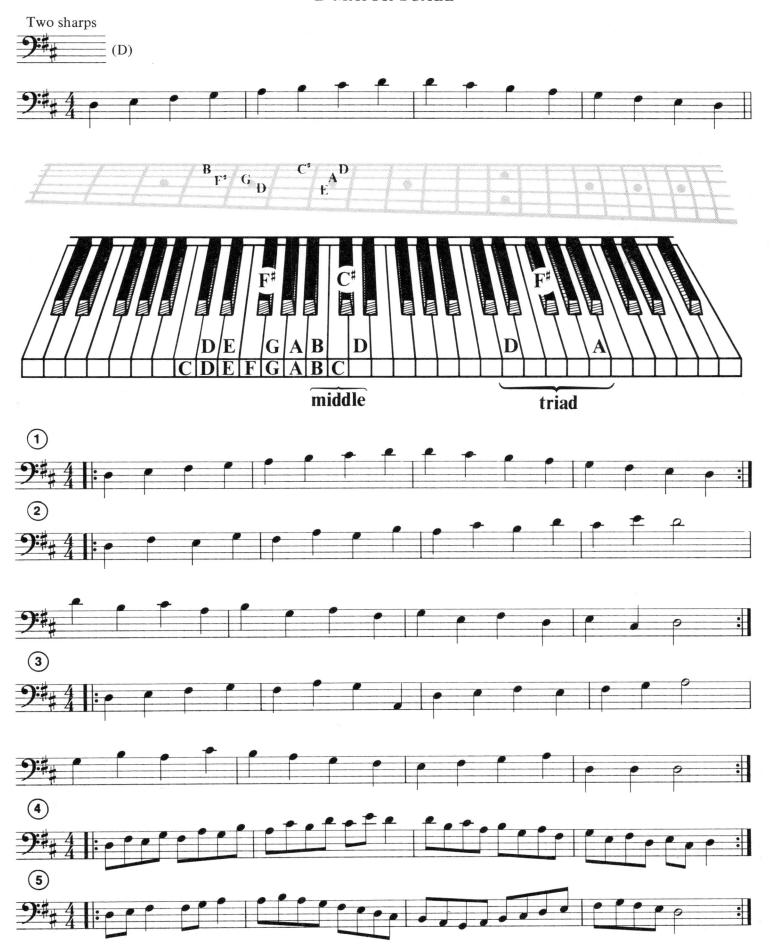

A MAJOR SCALE

E MAJOR SCALE

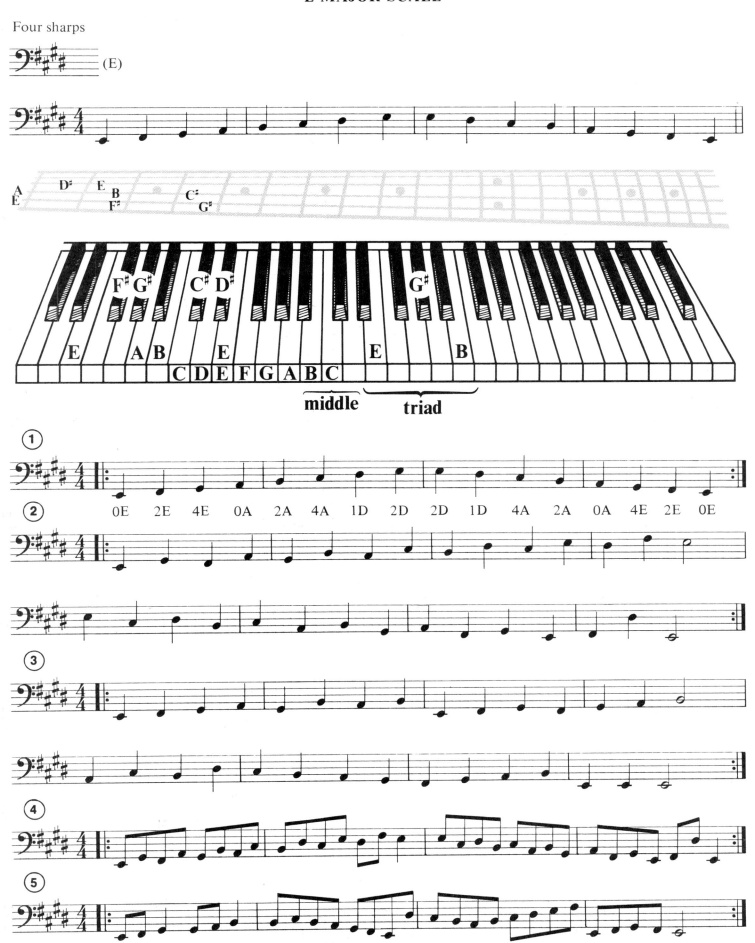

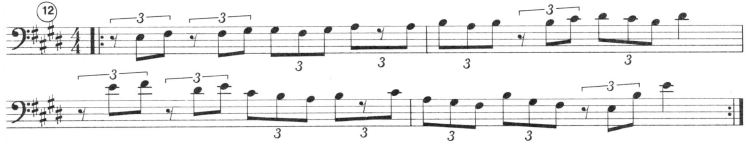

Extended range exercise in the key of E — Using another position on the fingerboard.

B MAJOR SCALE

F SHARP MAJOR SCALE

C SHARP MAJOR SCALE

Seven sharps

MAJOR AND DOMINANT SEVENTHS

Lowering the seventh degree of a scale or chord produces the characteristic DOMINANT SEVENTH sound.

This exercise covers the entire fingerboard and all MAJOR keys; and demonstrates tonal difference between the MAJOR SEVENTH and DOMINANT SEVENTH sound.

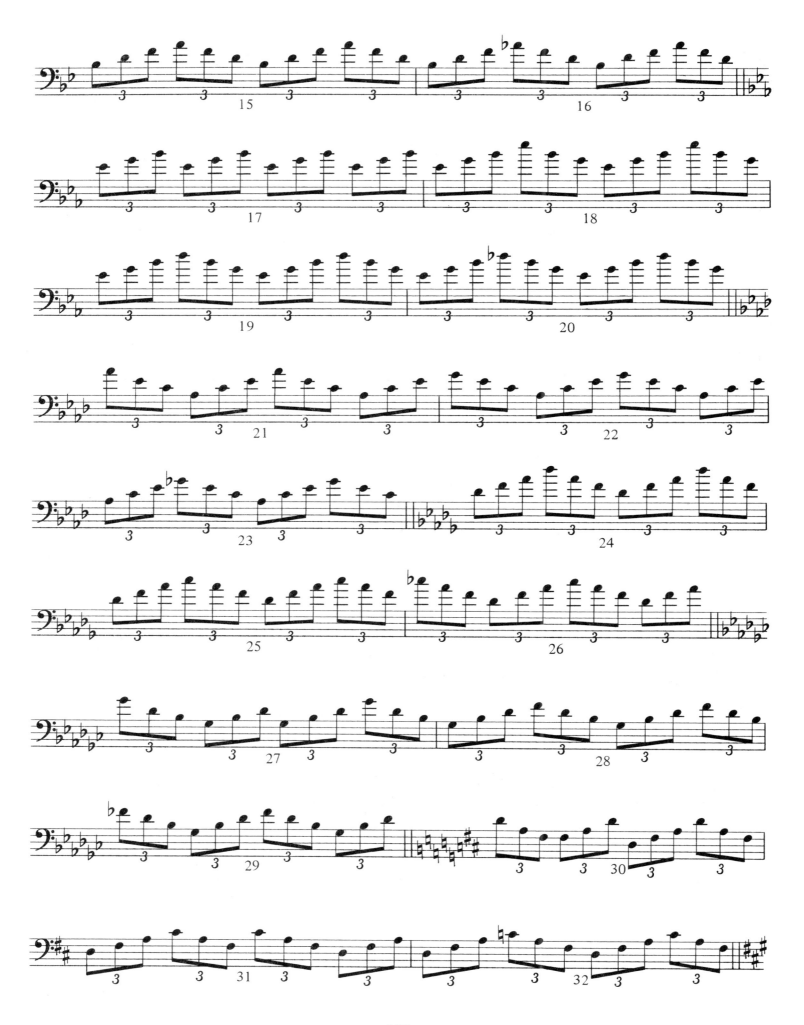

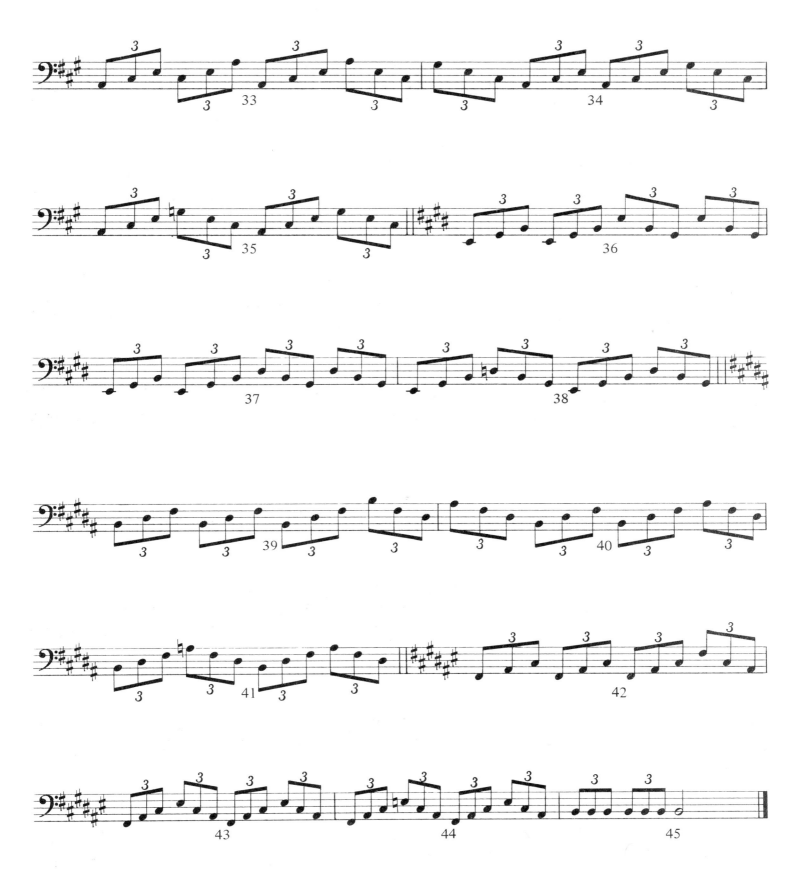

You can also use this exercise to test the action of your bass, a borrowed bass, a new bass, etc.; test the effects in intonation of any fret wear on the neck of the instrument.

Chapter Four

Minor Scales

NATURAL MINOR SCALES

A *minor scale* requires the key signature of the major scale three semitones higher. For example, C minor uses the key signature of E♭ major (three flats). Major and minor scales using the same key signature are related. (C minor is the *relative* minor of E♭ major).

FINGERING THE NATURAL MINOR SCALES

The following chart shows the relationship of the written C minor scale to the piano keyboard and the fingerboard of the electric bass. There are two basic ways to finger the minor scales. To best facilitate a definite process by which you can begin playing these scales, we will use one basic method of fingering (with a few exceptions).

The sequence of eight numbers (1 3 4 1 3 4 1 3) represents a practical and intelligent procedure for playing the eight musical notes that comprise each natural minor scale.

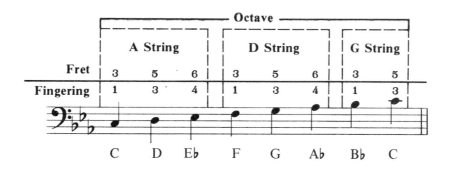

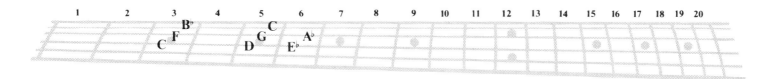

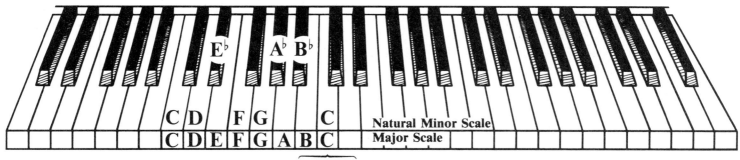

MINOR SCALE AND
KEY SIGNATURE PLACEMENT

The following NATURAL MINOR scales show the relationship of MINOR scales to their MAJOR key signature, and offer a basic MINOR scale exercise in fourteen keys. Two exercises follow the fourteen scales and should be memorized in all keys for use as a practice and study aid for all the NATURAL MINOR scales.

Note: Fingering suggested for No. 1 and 8 are in open string positions. However, the A Minor Scale (No. 1) can also be played using the fingering described on page 152 beginning the scale on the 5th fret of the E String.

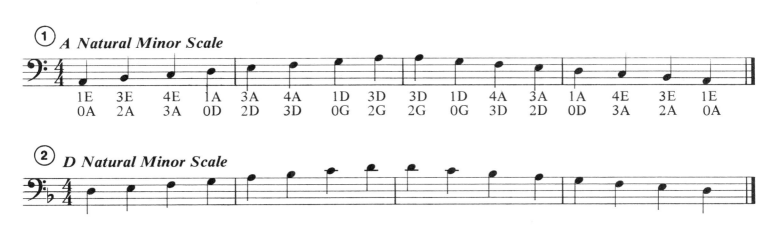

① *A Natural Minor Scale*

| 1E | 3E | 4E | 1A | 3A | 4A | 1D | 3D | 3D | 1D | 4A | 3A | 1A | 4E | 3E | 1E |
| 0A | 2A | 3A | 0D | 2D | 3D | 0G | 2G | 2G | 0G | 3D | 2D | 0D | 3A | 2A | 0A |

② *D Natural Minor Scale*

③ *G Natural Minor Scale*

④ *C Natural Minor Scale*

⑤ *F Natural Minor Scale*

⑥ *B Flat Natural Minor Scale*

⑦ *E Flat Natural Minor Scale*

⑧ *E Natural Minor Scale*

0E 2E 3E 0A 2A 3A 0D 2D 2D 0D 3A 2A 0A 3E 2E 0E

⑨ *B Natural Minor Scale*

⑩ *F Sharp Natural Minor Scale*

⑪ *C Sharp Natural Minor Scale*

⑫ *G Sharp Natural Minor Scale*

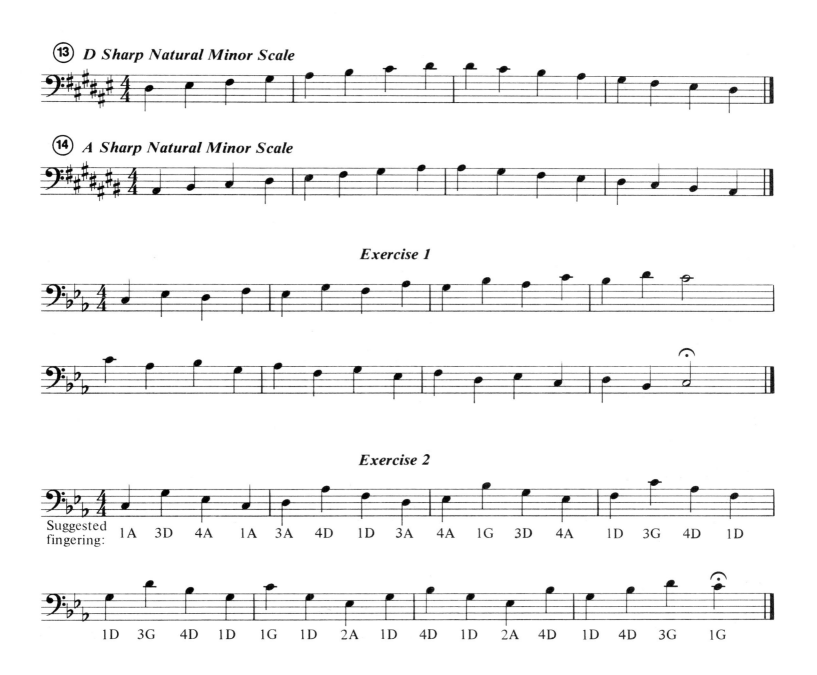

⑬ *D Sharp Natural Minor Scale*

⑭ *A Sharp Natural Minor Scale*

Exercise 1

Exercise 2

Suggested
fingering: 1A   3D   4A   1A   3A   4D   1D   3A   4A   1G   3D   4A   1D   3G   4D   1D

1D   3G   4D   1D   1G   1D   2A   1D   4D   1D   2A   4D   1D   4D   3G   1G

HARMONIC MINOR SCALES

A harmonic minor scale changes slightly. The leading tone (seventh degree of the scale) is raised a semitone/half tone, altering the sound of the scale/chord and the fingering of that note. With the exceptions of Rock and Rhythm & Blues, when music is written in a minor key, the harmonic scale is predominantly the basis of that key.

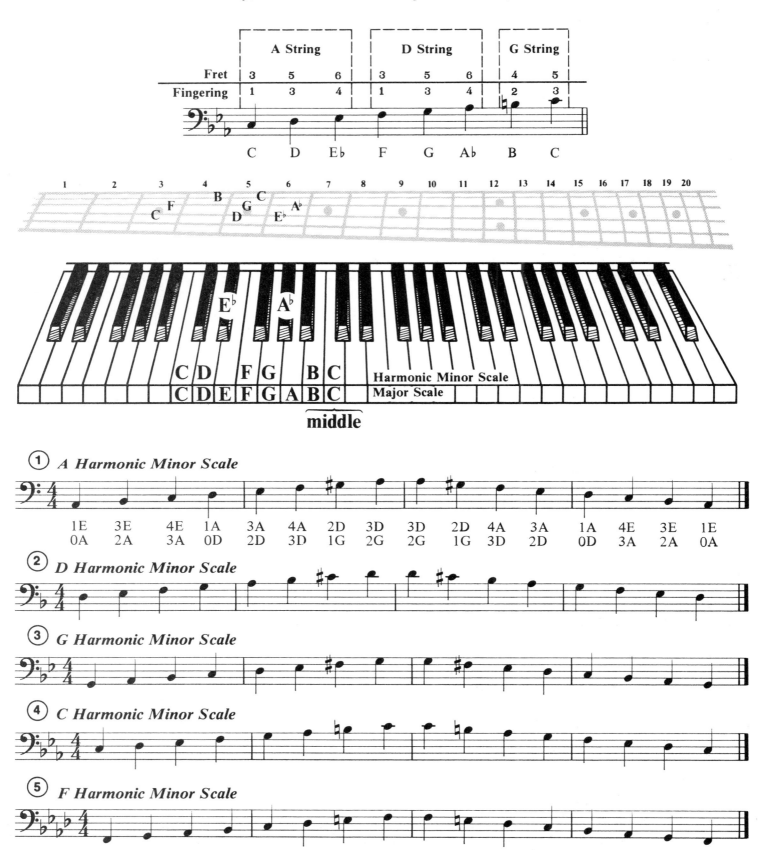

Exercise 1

Exercise 2

Exercise 3

Player 1 reads and repeats the top line of this eight measure exercise once (sixteen measures) and continues on to the bottom line after the second repeat.

Player 2 reads and repeats the bottom line of this eight measure exercise once (sixteen measures) and continues on to the top line after the second repeat.

MELODIC MINOR SCALES

A melodic scale is formed by raising both the sixth and seventh degrees a semitone/ half tone when ascending.

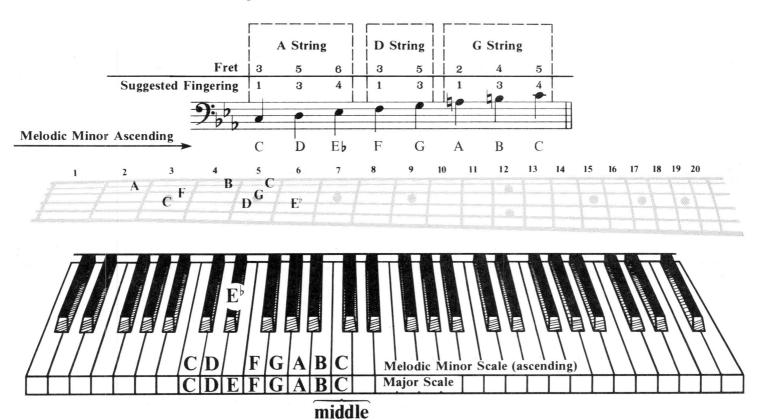

Melodic Minor Ascending →

Restore both notes to their original pitch and position in the key signature when descending. The fingering indicated is one of a few ways to finger the descending scale.

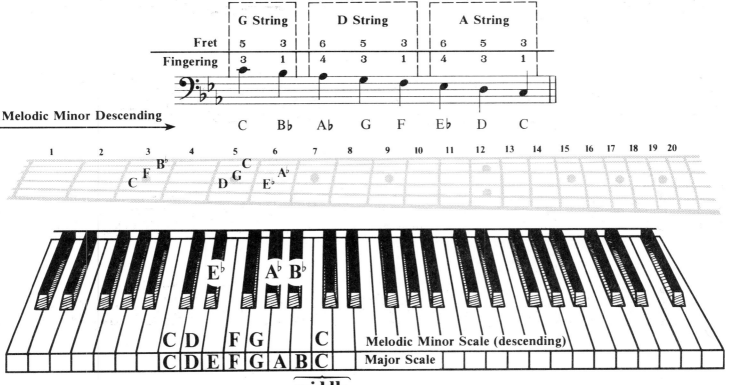

Melodic Minor Descending →

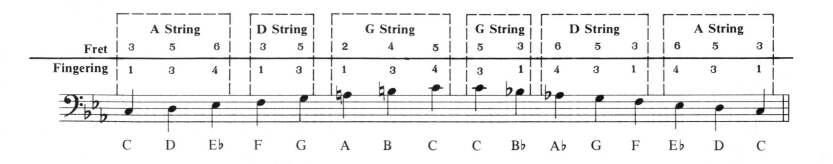

Fret	A String			D String		G String			G String		D String			A String		
	3	5	6	3	5	2	4	5	5	3	6	5	3	6	5	3
Fingering	1	3	4	1	3	1	3	4	3	1	4	3	1	4	3	1

C D Eb F G A B C C Bb Ab G F Eb D C

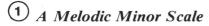

① *A Melodic Minor Scale*

1E 3E 4E 1A 3A 1D 3D 4D 3D 1D 4A 3A 1A 4E 3E 1E
0A 2A 3A 0D 2D 4D 1G 2G 2G 0G 3D 2D 0D 3A 2A 0A

② *D Melodic Minor Scale*

③ *G Melodic Minor Scale*

④ *C Melodic Minor Scale*

1A 3A 4A 1D 3D 1G 3G 4G 3G 1G 4D 3D 1D 4A 3A 1A

⑤ *F Melodic Minor Scale*

1E 3E 4E 1A 3A 0D 2D 3D 3D 1D 4A 3A 1A 4E 3E 1E

⑥ *B Flat Melodic Minor Scale*

—160—

Exercise 1

Exercise 2

Exercise 3

Player 1 reads and repeats the top line of this eight measure exercise once (sixteen measures) and continues on to the bottom line after the second repeat.

Player 2 reads and repeats the bottom line of this eight measure exercise once (sixteen measures) and continues on to the top line after the second repeat.

CHROMATIC MINOR SEVENTH
SCALE EXERCISES

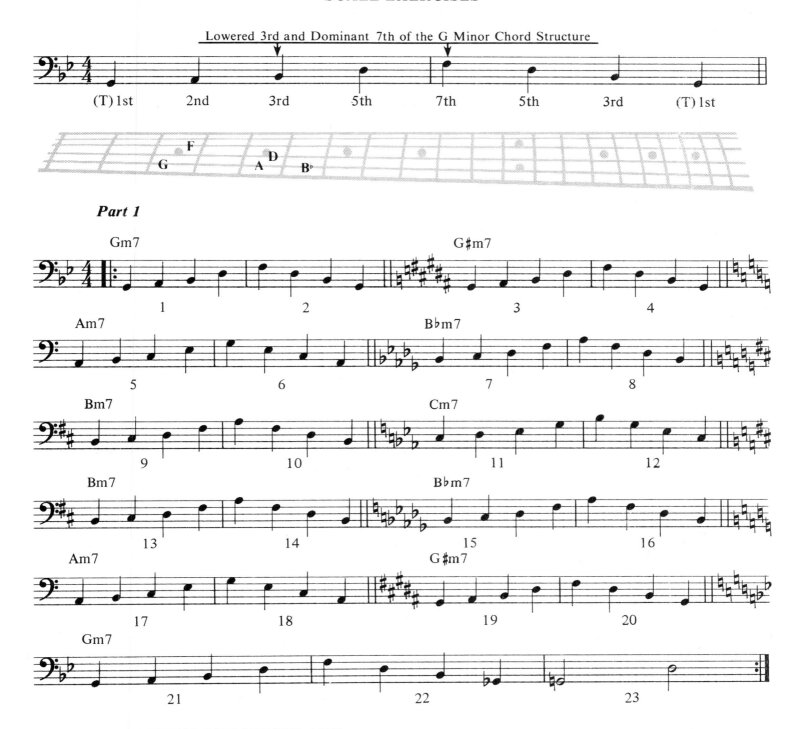

FOR STUDY, MEMORIZE AND
    Play exercise using eighth notes.
    Begin exercise on open E string using quarter notes.
    Begin exercise on open E string using eighth notes.

Part 2

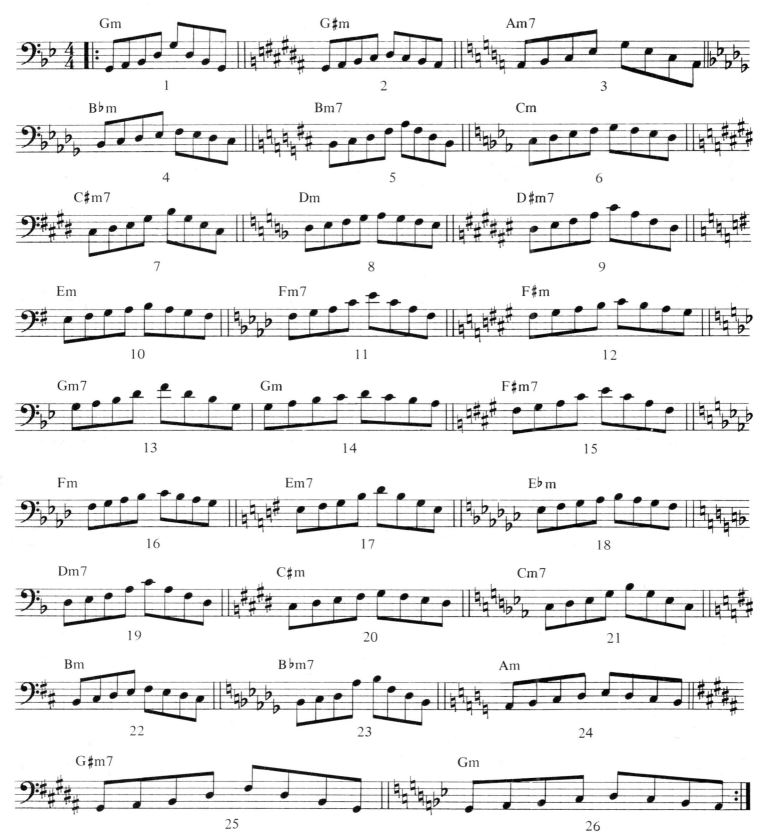

FOR STUDY, MEMORIZE AND
    Play exercise using sixteenth notes.
    Begin exercise on open E string using eighth notes and then sixteenth notes.
    Using the above formats, play exercise without using any open strings
    (except E).

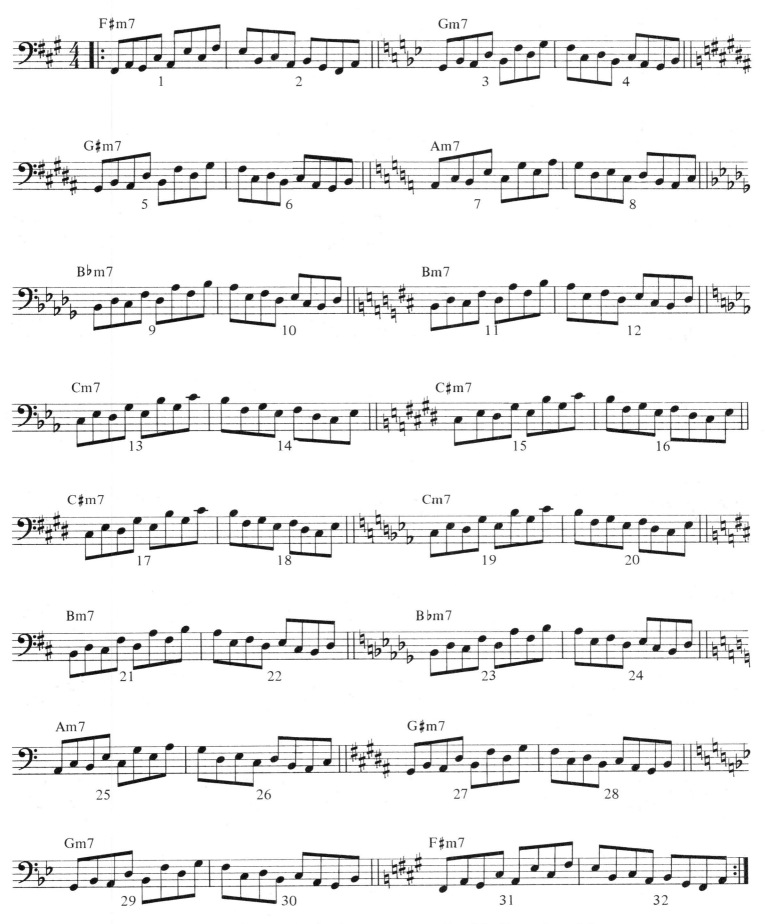

Part 3

Memorize and use this exercise in the manner outlined in Parts 1 and 2.

Part 4

This exercise moves chromatically in two measure phrases and is an excellent study exercise for strengthening and training the hand to hold a secure and stable fingering position.

First, practice and study the exercise by beginning each two measure phrase on the E string (ascending and descending). Second, practice and study the exercise by shifting to the A string at measure eleven and continue the exercise on the A string.

PARALLEL SCALES

The following major and minor scales, in groups of two, use the same letter name for their tonic note and are theoretically known as parallel to each other.

④ E Flat Major

E Flat Natural Minor

⑤ A Flat Major

A Flat Natural Minor

⑥ D Flat Major

C Sharp Natural Minor/D Flat Natural Minor

NOTE: The C sharp natural minor scale is fingered and pitched the same as the
D flat natural minor scale.

⑦ G Flat Major

F Sharp Natural Minor/G Flat Natural Minor

NOTE: The F sharp natural minor scale is fingered and pitched the same as the G flat
natural minor scale.

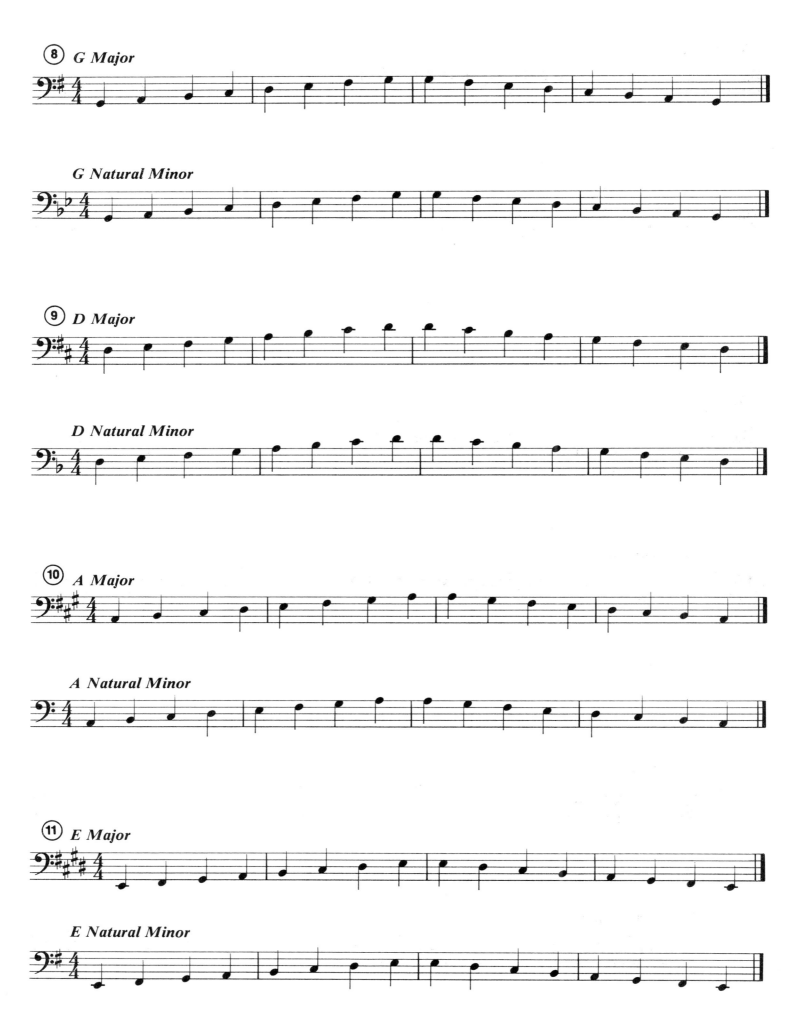

12 *B Major*

B Natural Minor

13 *F Sharp Major*

F Sharp Natural Minor

14 *C Sharp Major*

C Sharp Natural Minor

RELATIVE SCALES

The following major and minor scales use the same key signature and are theoretically known as relative to each other.

G flat natural minor is usually notated as F sharp natural minor using the key signature of A major.

D flat natural minor is usually notated as C sharp natural minor using the key signature of E major.

B Major

G Sharp Natural Minor

A flat natural minor is usually notated as G sharp natural minor using the key signature of B major.

13 **F Sharp Major**

D Sharp Natural Minor

14 **C Sharp Major**

A Sharp Natural Minor

Chapter Five

Diminished Scales

Diminished scales, arpeggios and chords are all minor 3rd inversions and are obtained by lowering the 3rd and 5th degrees of the major scale that is in use.

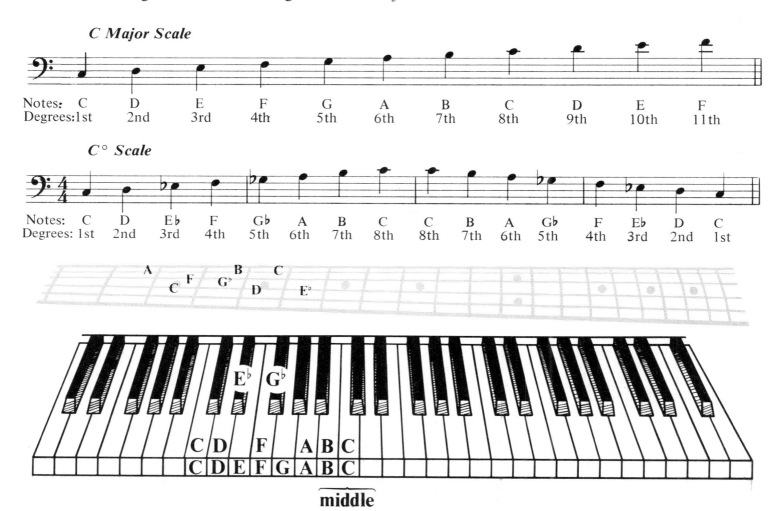

On the following pages, the first line of each scale is spelled harmonically and agrees with the diminished theory. The second line *a* of each scale is spelled enharmonically to show the choice of two notes that sound the same. The third line *b* of each example represents an arpeggio spelled so as to facilitate easier reading.

For instance, the F diminished scale and/or arpeggio is obtained by lowering the 3rd and 5th degrees of its scale (the notes A and C are lowered to A♭ and C♭). C♭ agrees with the diminished theory in this key and is harmonic to the scale; however, B sounds the same and is fingered the same.

The following diminished arpeggios are in two measure phrases ascending and descending chromatically. After reading the exercise, memorize the pattern and format for study use.

THE TRITONE

The sound of a tritone helps to distinguish the sound of a diminished arpeggio or chord from that of the major, minor, and augmented structures. The intervals of a tritone span three whole tones from the root.

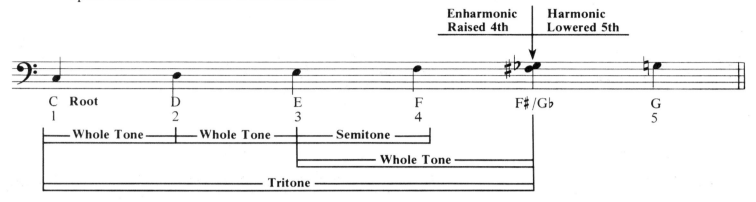

If C is the root, C to D equals a whole tone, D to E equals a whole tone, and E to F# equals a whole tone; therefore, the tritone of the note C is F#. Moving from C to F# is a diminished sound. F#/Gb are the same note; F# is the raised fourth and is enharmonic to the diminished scale, whereas Gb is the lowered fifth and is harmonic to the scale.

C Diminished Scale (C°)

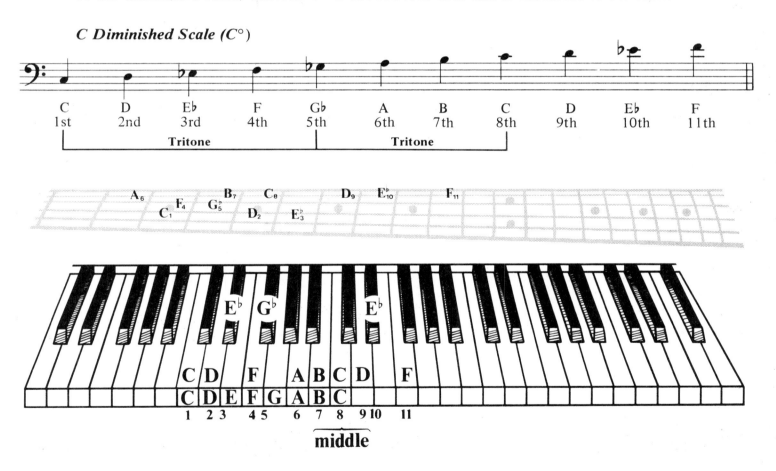

AUGMENTED SCALES

Augmented scales, arpeggios and chords are all major 3rd inversions and are obtained by raising the 5th degree of the major scale that is in use.

Notes:	C	D	E	F	G	A	B	C	D	E	F
Degrees:	1st	2nd	3rd	4th	5th	6th	7th	8th	9th	10th	11th

① C+ scale

Fingering: 2A 4A 1D 2D 1G 1G 3G 4G 4G 3G 1G 1G 2D 1D 4A 2A
4D 4D

①a C+ arpeggio

4E 3A 2D 1G 4G 1G 2D 3A 4E 1G 2D 3A 1G 2D 3A 4E

② F+ scale

1E 3E 0A 1A 4A 0D 2D 3D 3D 2D 0D 4A 1A 0A 3E 1E

②a F+ arpeggio

1E 0A 4A 2D 0G 2D 4A 0A 1E 3D 4A 0A 3D 4A 0A 1E

③ Bb+ scale

③a Bb+ arpeggio

④ Eb+ scale

④a Eb arpeggio

4E 3A 2D 1G 4G 1G 2D 3A 4E 1G 2D 3A 1G 2D 3A 4E
3A 2D 1G 4G 4G 4G 1G 2D 3A 4G 1G 2D 4G 1G 2D 3A

EXERCISES

DYNAMIC EXPRESSIONS OF FORCE

Crescendo (cresc.)   Gradually louder
Decrescendo (decresc.)   Gradually softer
Dolce   Sweetly
Dolcissimo   Very softly and sweetly
Forte *(f)*   Loud
Fortissimo *(ff)*   Very loud
Fortississimo *(fff)*   Extremely loud
Mezzo *(m)*   Medium
Mezzo forte *(mf)*   Medium loud
Mezzo piano *(mp)*   Medium soft
Piano *(p)*   Softly
Pianissimo *(pp)*   Very soft
Pianississimo *(ppp)*   Extremely soft
Sforzando, Sforzato *(sfz)*   Strongly accented

SIGNS AND ABBREVIATED EXPRESSIONS

Fermata 🎵   This sign over a note or rest means the note or rest is held as long as you or the leader (conductor) wishes.

Dal segno 𝄋 **D.S.**   First you will see the sign (𝄋), continue through the music until you see the letters (D.S.). These letters abbreviate dal segno—meaning: return to sign (𝄋) seen earlier in the composition.

Da capo *D.C.*   Go back to the beginning.

Octave change *8va*   Play music an octave higher.
8vb   Play music an octave lower.

Coda sign ⊕   When this sign first appears in the composition, continue on — obey the D.S. or D.C. The next time you arrive at the Coda sign (⊕), skip to the last part of the composition marked Coda.

Simile (similar)   Term indicating that a phrase is to be played in the same manner as the phrase preceding it.

ACCENT MARKS

($\downarrow$) ($\dot{\mathsf{r}}$)   A dot above or below the note means the note is to be played short.

($\underline{\downarrow}$) ($\bar{\mathsf{r}}$)   A tenuto above or below the note means to draw the note out.

($\underset{\vee}{\downarrow}$) ($\overset{\wedge}{\mathsf{r}}$)   A short crisp accent.

($\underset{>}{\downarrow}$) ($\overset{>}{\mathsf{r}}$)   A normal accent mark.

($\underset{\pm}{\downarrow}$) ($\overset{\pm}{\mathsf{r}}$)   Slap (wood sound) accent mark. (See Book 2).

MUSICAL TERM MARKINGS

Accelerando — Gradually increasing the speed
Adagio — Very slow
Ad Lib. (Ad libitum) — At your own liberty
Allegro — Fast
Andante — Moderately slow
Poco a poco — Little by little
A tempo — Return to the previous tempo
Grave — Very slow and solemnly
Largo — Slow and stately
Legato — Bound together, play smoothly and connected

Lento — Very slow
L'istesso — In the same time
Moderato — Play at a moderate speed or tempo
Prestissimo — As fast as possible
Presto — Very fast
Rallentando (rall.) — Gradually slower
Ritardando (rit.) — A gradual slowing of the tempo
Rubato — To skip or steal the tempo
Tempo — Rate of speed
Vivace — With life

Index